SECRETS UNCOVERED

LEONARD BRAND

SECRETS UNCOVERED

STORIES FROM
A CHRISTIAN
FOSSIL
HUNTER

Pacific Press®
Publishing Association
Nampa, Idaho | www.pacificpress.com

Cover design by Steve Lanto
Cover design resources provided by author
Interior design by Aaron Troia
Interior photos provided by the author

The author assumes full responsibility of all facts and quotations as cited in this book.

Unless otherwise noted, Bible quotations are from the King James Version.

Bible quotations marked TLB are taken from *The Living Bible* copyright © 1971 by Tyndale House Foundation. Used by permission of Tyndale House Publishers Inc., Carol Stream, Illinois 60188. All rights reserved.

Scripture quotations marked NIV are taken from the HOLY BIBLE, NEW INTERNATIONAL VERSION®. Copyright © 1973, 1978, 1984, 2011 by Biblica, Inc.® Used by permission. All rights reserved worldwide.

Scripture marked NKJV is taken from the New King James Version®. Copyright © 1982 by Thomas Nelson. Used by permission. All rights reserved.

Additional copies of this book are available for purchase by calling toll-free 1-800-765-6955 or by visiting adventistbookcenter.com.

ISBN 978-0-8163-6520-3

February 2020

CONTENTS

Preface 7

Chapter 1 A Journey Begins 9

Chapter 2 Trails in the Grand Canyon 15

Chapter 3 Plodding Salamanders Will Try Your Patience 24

Chapter 4 Did Humans Walk With Dinosaurs? 33

Chapter 5 The Argument, the Windstorm, and the Turtle Hunt 40

Chapter 6 Headless Turtles and Suburban Surprises 49

Chapter 7 Return to Cedar Mountain 57

Chapter 8 Don't Let the Rocks Get the Best of You 66

Chapter 9 Lakes, Turtles, and Volcanoes 73

Chapter 10 Do You Want to See Some Fossil Whales? 79

Chapter 11 Disarticulating Jeeps and Beautiful, Articulated Fernanda 89

Chapter 12 Sergio 97

Chapter 13   Sergio and the Spaniard's Wife   106

Chapter 14   Mother's Day Robbers and the Five-Star Hotel   111

Chapter 15   Who Cares About Fossil Whales?   117

Chapter 16   Sergio and the Devil   122

Chapter 17   God Helped You Again!   129

Chapter 18   Bodyguards and Fossil Thieves   138

Chapter 19   Screenmeisters in Wyoming   145

Chapter 20   New Questions and Rattlesnakes in Utah   153

Chapter 21   Learning to Trust God's Guidance   163

Chapter 22   Bedded Rocks and Flying Saucers   172

Chapter 23   Take to the Air   180

Chapter 24   "You Do Have a Different Search Image"   188

Chapter 25   A Vision for the Future   195

Chapter 26   What to Do Next?   203

Afterword   Foundation for a Life   211

References   215

PREFACE

Exploration and discovery have been the center of my work as a paleontologist. What I discovered in this pursuit is that a Christian perspective is not, as some would claim, a hindrance to being a productive scientist but can actually be an advantage in that work, even in geology and paleontology.

I could never have anticipated the fascination that has flowed out of this journey through the pages of fossil history. Our Creator gave us an outline of earth history, but He valued the human desire to look and find new things (new to us), so He left innumerable details for us to discover.

The stories in this book provide a glimpse into what it is like to work as a field paleontologist/geologist, with both the human and the scholarly sides of being a scientist. The primary scientists who led out in this research all have doctoral degrees and are experienced scientists who are employed at various academic institutions and who publish papers in scientific research journals. Some names and a few situations have been changed to provide anonymity for certain individuals and to keep the stories from being excessively long. Otherwise, all the events in these stories happened just as they are described.

I wish to thank all those who have shared this journey with me. In modern science, one person can seldom do it alone—high-quality research work comes as a team effort. I also thank our great God, who was with us all the way. May He be honored by our efforts. Thanks to Ken McFarland and Tim Lale for reading and improving the manuscript.

1

A JOURNEY BEGINS

During my undergrad years, I took a class on biological origins from Lloyd Downs, a professor of biology at La Sierra College (now La Sierra University), in which he compared creationist and non-creationist views of earth history. The topic was fascinating to me, and I determined then that I would contribute to this challenging field somehow. I had no idea how it would happen.

Perhaps, I thought, I could honor the Creator as a scientist employed in some museum, showing that a believer can do high-quality scientific work. I remember sitting in a business meeting of the American Society of Mammalogists, watching the society president and thinking, *Will I need to be up there in that position someday in order to honor God?*

I knew one thing for sure: I would never be a teacher. I could not imagine myself ever giving lectures to a room full of people.

While earning a master's degree in biology at Loma Linda University (LLU) in Southern California, I decided on Cornell University in upstate New York as the best place to study for a doctorate in biology. I became acquainted with Dr. McClain, a biology professor, and my future advisor at Cornell. My parents were very supportive of advanced education but reminded me they didn't have the money to finance my continued graduate work. I put my optimism to work and applied to the National Science Foundation (NSF) for a graduate fellowship to fund my doctoral studies.

The scene is still etched in my memory—I sat in the LLU campus snack bar on a Sunday morning after I found in my mailbox an envelope from the NSF. I ate a leisurely breakfast before opening the envelope because, having received the fat envelope and not the skinny rejection letter, I knew it meant the NSF had granted me a fellowship for my doctoral program.

That summer, after finishing my master's degree, I had an opportunity to take a six-week field course in paleontology. It required a choice between dating a girl who interested me or taking the class. I chose the class—and someone else married the girl.

The summer class traveled from Texas through Colorado, Wyoming, Utah, and Arizona, studying rocks and fossils and discussing how the biblical story of earth history can explain the evidence. On this trip, we had opportunities to hunt for fossils.

My road to becoming a paleontologist was not a smooth journey. For some unknown reason, I seemed to be the person who had trouble finding fossils, and I concluded that paleontology was fascinating but perhaps not the right field for me. After an unsuccessful hunt for fossil fish near Fossil, Wyoming (now part of Fossil Butte National Monument), I sneaked away from the group, got out my shotgun, and collected, skinned, and stuffed a chipmunk—something I could do better than finding those elusive fossils!

A vivid memory from that trip was the night we camped on top of Polecat Bench, a rich fossil locality in Wyoming, with little fossil skulls "all over the place"—or so we were told. A fierce wind began blowing during the night, not leaving much possibility for sleep. In the morning, we carefully got up, holding our sleeping bags with one hand and pants with the other so they wouldn't be blown across the prairie to South Dakota. We did get to see fellow student Gershon running across Polecat Bench after the lid to his ice chest as it soared gracefully out of reach over the sagebrush. To this day, the name Polecat Bench suggests to me an aura of something wild and full of potential and yet unpleasant.

I learned later that when a vertebrate paleontologist says a fossil site has fossil skulls *all over the place*, that usually means he searched all day and found three or four little skulls (where I found none).

After the Wyoming trip, I started across the country in a Volkswagen Beetle full of my belongings with thirty dollars in my pocket. My hope was to get to Cornell and find my first NSF fellowship check before running out of money. That trip was feasible at the time, with gasoline at twenty-nine cents a gallon. I arrived in Ithaca, New York, and spent the first night in a motel room for about five dollars. The clerk questioned me when I said that I would be the only one in the room. It seems they got that story often from students when there would actually be two in the room—my first indication that the values there were different from mine.

The next morning it became evident that Cornell was not the friendly little place Loma Linda University had been. The administrator insistently followed a set plan, and I would not get my first fellowship check for several weeks.

It was raining hard that day, and after spending a few dollars for supper, I walked along under the shelter of a mall canopy, wondering what to do about my thin wallet. My last dollar went for a call home to ask my parents to send some money, which my beloved father was happy to do the next day. The problem remained that evening as to where I could spend the night. I drove north along Cayuga Lake to Taughannock Falls State Park and drove into the parking lot. Setting up a tent in the driving rain didn't seem inviting, so I slept sitting up in the front seat of my VW, among all my earthly belongings. That parking lot, it turned out, was a favorite place for student couples to park and "watch the submarine races," which made it all the more lonely for me.

My doctoral studies were in ecology and evolutionary biology. It turned out that it wasn't possible for me to get away from the fossils, as my graduate advisor spent a lot of time on vertebrate paleontology in his vertebrate biology classes. That was a good introduction, as it turned out, to areas of future study for me.

The three faculty members on my guidance committee were supportive, and I had a good relationship with my advisor, who was very friendly. When he came down the hall past my student office, he would stop to say hello and chat a little.

I had things all planned out in my mind to eventually deal with my unwillingness to attend classes on Saturday, which is my Sabbath, but not until the teachers knew and respected me and would not be so bothered by such issues. It seemed like a good plan, but it didn't work out that way. By the end of the first week, it became clear that my advisor's mammalogy lab would be on Saturday. Friday afternoon, with considerable palpitation of heart, I went to his office and explained the situation.

"That's not a problem," he said. "The lab material will still be out on Sunday, and you can study it then." However, he no longer stopped by to say hello when he passed my office, and not to be on speaking terms with your advisor is not good news in graduate school. The problem was not only my habit of observing the Sabbath. Once he knew my religious views, he also knew I was a creationist.

As winter set in, the weather turned very cold in upstate New York. One morning I drove to school and parked in the lot beside the football practice field. To reduce the amount of time spent walking in the bitter ten-degree weather, I cut across the football field and up a steep bank covered with about two feet of snow. The bank was slippery, and I stepped and shuffled up the fifteen-foot-high slope. In the classroom, I discovered my keys were not in my pocket—they must have fallen out somewhere on the steep bank. The thought of trying to deal with lost keys under those winter conditions was very discouraging to me, only adding to the weight of the still-discouraging relations with my advisor.

I prayed as I went out to look for the keys. At the top of the slope, the situation looked bleak, just like my mood. My tracks up the slope were evident, but I thought the keys could be anywhere under the deep snow. I would have to try searching anyway, and reluctantly I began the search right there at the top of the slope. My hand went down, seemingly forever, through the snow, and on that first try, it closed around the keys! God knew I needed encouragement that day. My advisor noticed my obvious happiness as I reentered the classroom, but I didn't have the courage to tell him why I was so jubilant.

After about a month, my advisor became friendly again. It's possible the change came after he read my LLU master's thesis, which he thought was well done. He suggested I write up part of it and submit it for the "best student paper" competition at the upcoming American Society of Mammalogists annual meetings. I did write the paper—and won the award. This increased my appreciation for Professor Ryckman at Loma Linda, who had pushed me to do so much work on that master's thesis, beyond what seemed necessary at the time.

Loma Linda University, where Leonard Brand is employed.

The Cornell years rolled by, and finally, it was time to defend my doctoral dissertation on a cold day in December. The exam would decide the outcome of three years of graduate study. My three guidance committee members and I sat in a circle in the Laboratory of Ornithology while they asked many questions. In spite of the tension of the moment, pleasantness prevailed, with a lovely winter scene outside the window, and inside, three gentlemanly professors who had become my friends.

The exam was not a pushover. I had to defend my research and convince my professors that the evidence supported my conclusions about chipmunk biology. They accepted my dissertation and the rest of my graduate work, even though I was a creationist—and it was finished!

That Friday evening, waiting outside a hotel for friends to take me to a meeting at my church, I entertained myself by running and sliding on the icy sidewalk. I was wondering, *Are PhDs supposed to act this way?* But I didn't care—the doctoral study was completed, and I was happy.

About two years after I came to Loma Linda, Harold Coffin brought me a handful of scientific papers on ancient fossilized reptile tracks in Arizona and asked if I would give a short report on them at some meetings.

"Sure," I said, not having any idea of the journey that was beginning. In time, I would learn a whole new field—geology—through taking geology classes and in field research with geologists.

2

TRAILS IN THE GRAND CANYON

The life of a paleontologist is filled with stories of personal research adventures in the wilderness, and every landscape and fossil has a story behind it—a story of how it came to be formed and preserved. The search for these stories keeps us coming back year after year. How much can we know about how a particular fossil got there? What approach can help us most in this search? Harold Coffin's papers on animal tracks were intriguing and puzzling to me. My central question was, How could those fossils be consistent with the Bible story of the flood?

If you've been to the Grand Canyon, you may have noticed a broad, white, horizontal band of rock near the top of the canyon walls. That band is known as the Coconino Sandstone, three hundred feet thick. When geologists first study a new region and name a newly discovered body of rock, typically they name it after a local town or other landmark. The Coconino Sandstone, known as the Coconino SS, was given an Indian name, perhaps after the Coconino Plateau south of the Grand Canyon.

The trackways mentioned in Coffin's papers were set in the Coconino SS. To picture how the trackways got there, at least according to the standard scientific explanation, imagine an extensive desert covered with sand dunes, with the wind carrying sand and dropping it on the lee, or downwind, side of each dune. This process causes the dunes to grow in the downwind direction, forming one sloping layer after another on the surface of the dunes. Most geologists think this is how the Coconino SS was formed long ago. Reptiles walked over these dunes in the cool of the morning, stalking scorpions and spiders, and all these creatures left tracks in the sand. But does this fit with the Bible account of the great flood?

The Grand Canyon in Arizona. The white band near
the top of the cliff is the Coconino Sandstone.

In one spot in the Coconino SS, a beautiful fossil track is visible today, left by a small invertebrate animal that meandered across one slab of the sandstone. A larger animal, a reptile, comes in from the side, and their tracks meet. We are seeing fossilized behavior, like a single still frame from a video. At the point where the two tracks meet, there is evidence of a little scurrying action, and only the reptile track continues on. It appears that someone was eaten on that very spot several thousand years ago!

The sandstone is a series of stacked horizontal sets, each several feet thick, containing many of the original sloping layers of sand. This layering is called cross-bedded sandstone. After the sand accumulated, groundwater seeping through the spaces between the sand grains brought chemicals that cemented it into sandstone. The only fossils in the Coconino SS are the animal tracks.

As I thought about how to present the content of Coffin's papers, I wondered how to relate this desert environment to the biblical global flood. The Bible doesn't tell us the whole story—how many of the rock layers in the geological column were formed during the Flood, how many came after the Flood, or whether some actually formed before the Flood. It did seem likely to me that the Coconino SS was a candidate for formation during the Flood, but how could we determine if that were true? And how can we know the environment in which it formed? Are there feasible alternatives to a desert environment for forming this type of cross-bedded sandstone with its animal tracks? The scientific literature used the tracks as evidence to assert that the sandstone was indeed a desert, wind-blown deposit—but I wondered.

I concluded that additional significant questions remained. How would we know if the track-makers were correctly identified as reptiles, scorpions, and spiders? Are they identified as such because the sandstone is desert sand, or is the sandstone considered a desert deposit because we know the creatures were desert animals? This is an intertwined set of questions that were begging for answers.

But, you may be thinking, the previously published assertion that Coconino SS is a wind-created desert deposit unrelated to a flood was all decided by the scientific process, so why would I be questioning the published scientific facts?

I could decide to assume that since the Bible tells us there was a global flood, this sandstone was obviously formed in the Flood, under water, and therefore those other scientists are wrong. But I have never found the term *Coconino SS* in my Bible. The Bible gives us basic principles and leaves many details for us to figure out, such as how the Coconino SS was formed. Would the evidence challenge my belief in the Flood?

As I have thought about such questions, I have realized that we don't need to be afraid of research and evidence. We can trust the Bible. Ultimately, the truth doesn't need our protection, because truth can defend itself. Perhaps that is true even in the area of geology. Also, science has been quite successful in its endeavors, so it seems unwise to discount everything it has to say.

That idea can leave me a little uncomfortable, however. After all, many people have abandoned the Bible because they are convinced that science has disproved what the Bible says. It is important to trust God and to believe His Word, and the Bible also says we are to love God with not only all of our hearts but also with all of our minds. That seems to say we must trust—but also think.

So what is the answer? I decided to go out and follow those fossil footprints for a while. Perhaps they would lead to an answer to the dilemma.

Even if we question the conclusions of other scientists, it is necessary to read their scientific papers to know what they found, so we will know what to look for as we try to decide whether we agree with their interpretation of the evidence. In the early 1900s, Charles Gilmore and his field crew from the Smithsonian Institution came to the Grand Canyon and collected fossil tracks. After I had read their papers and hiked where they worked, I could almost see them still at their task along the canyon walls. The other prominent student of the canyon's geology was Edwin McKee. He did much of the early research on rock formations in northern Arizona, and he was the one who initiated the theory that the Coconino sand accumulated in a desert. I began with McKee's publications as I acquainted myself with the Grand Canyon.

Over spring vacation 1976, I headed for the Grand Canyon with Arthur Chadwick, a fellow faculty member at LLU. Dr. Chadwick was studying a sandstone near the bottom of the Grand Canyon to learn how it was deposited. When we arrived, the colorful, snow-covered canyon walls—standing against the backdrop of dark storm clouds—was an unforgettable sight. After spending the night in our camper, we headed down to our research sites. Art began his hike to the bottom of the canyon, and I headed to the

Coconino SS, just a fourth of the way down. Obviously, I had made the best choice for a research topic!

The Hermit Trail is old and no longer maintained, but it was well built and is still in good condition. The trail was built by a company seeking income from visitors who rode mules down into the canyon. With its grand vistas of the canyon, the trail is an interesting hike, but as I maneuvered down some of the high rock steps built into the trail, I was glad not to be riding a mule.

As we hiked down the trail, we didn't see any fossil tracks in the upper half of the Coconino SS, just as Edwin McKee had said would be true. But then, farther down, the tracks appeared along the trail, sometimes in abundance. What were these animals that so frequently left their signature on the sand slopes? They would in time become old friends to us, yet somewhat elusive and not eager to give up their secrets.

Leonard Brand studying fossil footprints
in the Coconino Sandstone, circa 1976.

Other travelers made their way along the trail as we went. Many were well-prepared, experienced hikers, and some were not. The canyon walls are steep, and it is a long way from the top to the bottom of the canyon, with no water supply along most of the trails. The canyon is also like an upside-down mountain. The easier, downward part of the hike comes first, and then, when hikers are tired, they face the challenging trek back to the top. A hiker's life can depend on their good physical condition and also on careful planning, with lots of drinking water.

Fossil trackway in the Coconino Sandstone.

Late one afternoon, a student assistant and I met another hiker, and we understood better why a number of people die in the canyon each year. We had weathered a brief rain and then hiked a short way below the Coconino SS to Santa Maria Spring to see if we could find good water there. We did not, and as we rested by the "spring," a man came hiking down the trail, asking how far it was to the campground. The campground was another twelve miles away, at the bottom of the canyon—a vertical mile below the canyon rim. The man was carrying only one thing—a six-pack of beer! Perhaps the use of six-packs earlier in the day might explain his behavior. He evidently gave up the hike to the bottom and was seen the next morning headed back up the trail. On this occasion, the canyon was kind to him, as the weather was not very hot.

On another trip, my young student assistant was eager for a hike to the bottom of the canyon and back. I was not as enthusiastic about making that long journey in one day but didn't want to disappoint him. We prepared for the hike with what we hoped would be adequate food and water. The Bright Angel Trail has two sources of drinking water along the pathway, spaced at approximately equal intervals. So it's only necessary to carry enough water to hike between these watering places.

Leaving camp just before dawn, we reached the Colorado River at midday. While my assistant hiked a little farther to a bridge over the river, I rested and ate lunch. Then came the journey back up the steep trail. I chose a pace I could maintain steadily without stopping to rest. A group of several young men was on the trail at the same time I was. Their strategy was different from mine—they would pass me quickly and then stop to rest, and then they would repeat it. I caught up and passed them at each of their resting places. They turned out to be a kind and thoughtful group. When they stopped at one of their resting places, I didn't show up. One of them came back to see if I was all right. At an especially scenic spot along the trail, I had stopped to take pictures and enjoy the wonders of the canyon. I have not forgotten their thoughtfulness.

However, I had a problem that I didn't tell them about. Two of my containers of water were used up, and I opened the last one. To my horror, the water was filled with floating bits of debris! What could they be? The water was in a plastic peanut butter jar, and I realized that the cardboard seal in the lid had disintegrated into the water. The water was still drinkable but not inviting. It was some distance to the next spring, so it was good to know the water was there if I were desperate enough to drink it. Two turkey vultures were circling overhead. *They might as well circle somewhere else*, I thought. *I am not that far gone yet!*

The long uphill climb finally brought us to the canyon rim at dusk. Though the hike was memorable, I probably will not do it again soon. It would be more enjoyable as a two-day hike.

After returning to LLU, we defined some research questions. Concerning the intriguing trackways of small animals walking through the sand, we considered how we could know the conditions that prevailed when the tracks were made. We didn't have access to a time machine to go back and watch them in person. This is, of course, a significant problem in any study of ancient earth history.

What is the alternative? In the absence of a time machine, we depend on a study of modern analogues. These analogues are situations existing now that could be similar to conditions that existed in the ancient environment. We can study animal tracks made today in deserts or other environments and compare them with the fossil tracks and sediments. One modern environment may be similar enough to the fossil deposit to convince us that the modern analogue explains the formation of the fossils.

A university science professor is expected to pursue research projects to answer important questions, to mentor students in research, and to get papers published in scientific research journals. Scientists don't make money from those publications. But if they are successful, the reward is that the university allows them to keep their job! As we do research, in the back of our mind are always the questions: *Will this research project be successful? Can I get it published in a good journal?* An important aid to getting the research done is working with graduate students. Our part is to guide the students in learning how to do research, and our reward is the students' success and publishing papers co-authored by student and professor.

To help us study modern analogues of the sandstone formation, my graduate assistant built an elongated wooden box and partly filled it with sand in the shape of a sloping sand dune. We formed a similar dune in an aquarium. The next task was to find suitable animals to make tracks in the sand. A drive into the Coast Range in Southern California brought me through a plateau with delightful live oaks scattered across the grassy hills. In a deep valley was a stream with abundant salamanders (western newts). My fellow traveler on that trip was a bobcat, which didn't seem concerned about me. It was walking across the road when I arrived and again strolled across the road as I departed.

My collecting box eventually held a number of salamanders. Back in the lab, I would create modern analogues for dry desert sand and underwater sand. The salamanders could make tracks in the sand for me.

The sand in the artificial dune needed to match the small, uniform size and rounded shape of the sand grains in the Coconino SS. After some searching, I found just the right sand—the red, fine-grained sand weathered out from the Navajo Sandstone in southern Utah, which forms colorful sand dunes along the highway north of Kanab.

The salamanders, and some lizards we used, made fine tracks on my artificial sand dunes. Dr. McKee had done similar experiments, and he said salamanders don't walk on the bottom under the water but swim from place to place. Edwin McKee was a productive scientist, and I was questioning his conclusions. Would this project be successful? Or was I going down a blind alley? I tried placing the salamanders underwater, and they did walk and make tracks in the sand under the water. Dr. McKee must have missed something. It would take more investigation to settle the confusion that arose from that handful of papers Harold Coffin had given me.

$$\textcircled{3}$$

PLODDING SALAMANDERS
WILL TRY YOUR PATIENCE

Do you want an interesting afternoon? Don't spend it watching salamanders. They plod along at their own pace—and only when they want to.

This slow pace may help explain why one paleontologist reached a mistaken conclusion about salamanders. The paleontologist convinced the scientist Edwin McKee that salamanders don't walk on the bottom underwater but swim from place to place. That is why McKee, in his own trackway experiments, didn't try any underwater track observations but only studied tracks of live animals on dry, damp, or wet sand.

Up in the Coast Range foothills of California, I decided to test McKee's conclusion about swimming salamanders. While catching salamanders with a butterfly net, I sat and watched their behavior. After a couple of hours of these observations, I wrote in my notebook that the man was mostly right. It looked as though salamanders do walk on the bottom, but most of their locomotion is swimming.

I put away the net, took out my watch, and began counting how much time a salamander spent in each type of movement. As I said, you shouldn't expect to spend an exciting afternoon watching salamanders. With patience, I collected plenty of data, and it turned out that most of the salamanders' locomotion is, in fact, walking on the bottom of the pond. Why was my original conclusion wrong?

The reason for my mistake illustrates why scientists are so anxious to count and measure things. The human brain isn't made like a computer that can notice everything that occurs equally well. If it were, we would probably become quite confused by all the action around us. Our brain is made to notice things important to us and filter out much of the rest. When it comes to observing salamanders, the ones that catch our attention are those that swim to the surface for air and then swim back down. We are much less likely to notice the salamander slowly plodding along on the bottom under the water. Counting and measuring the two different behaviors helps overcome our tendency to notice only what is more conspicuous and miss the rest.

In my first observations of salamanders and lizards walking on laboratory-made sand dunes, it seemed to me that dry sand or underwater sand tracks wouldn't provide good explanations for the fossil tracks. Tracks on wet sand (but not underwater) seemed to offer more promise. But research must be thorough, or it can lead to wrong conclusions. After we watched more plodding salamanders on the red Utah sand in the lab, it became evident to us that on dry, sloping sand, the loose sand slides into the track and obscures the details. Damp sand doesn't preserve any decent tracks at all. Wet sand shows good details, but on a slope, the sand quickly changes from very wet lower down to much firmer, less wet sand as the animal goes uphill. This creates a rapidly changing trackway appearance, very different from the uniform fossil tracks at Coconino.

Tracks with footprint details, uniform along the entire trackway, were made underwater on the red Utah sand. In fact, the underwater tracks were the only tracks that offered a suitable analog for the fossil tracks. Since sand deposits made by flowing water can be very similar to desert sand dunes, an underwater origin of these fossil tracks should be considered.

After I had made many more patient observations of salamanders, it was time to write up a paper for publication in a scientific journal. Great experiments are of little use unless the rest of the world can benefit from them. And publishing also provides quality control. Like other scientists, I am human, and I might overlook some important detail. I want to know if I have made a mistake. A paper sent to a research journal for publication is sent to several reviewers who are experts in the field. They will analyze it and recommend either that it be published, that it needs improvement, or it should be rejected. The paper will not be published unless it meets an expected quality of logic and shows a coherent connection between the data and conclusions. This is science's peer review process.

I knew there was an additional uncertainty, however, because my conclusions challenged the accepted interpretation of the Coconino SS as a deposit of desert sand. Would my unconventional conclusions be accepted by other scientists? Was there hope of getting it published? I could not be sure.

Before sending the paper to a journal, I sought some expert advice. Reading the past papers on fossil tracks in scientific journals, I had noted a couple of scientists whose research made them especially qualified to evaluate my paper. I wrote to them and asked if they would read my manuscript and give their opinion of it before I sent it for publication. Two of them agreed to read it—one of them, Edwin McKee himself!

The very idea of having Edwin McKee read my paper made my heart beat a little faster. Nevertheless, he read it and agreed that my observations supported my conclusions. He also sort of apologized for his friend who had said salamanders don't walk underwater. The other reader, Dr. William Sarjeant, liked the paper and asked me to present it as part of a symposium he was coordinating at national geology meetings to be held in Washington, DC, that same year. I agreed to present at the meeting.

When the time came for the trip across the country to the conference, my wife and one-year-old son, Dennis, accompanied me on the trip, which combined several things into one. After packing our camper van, we headed for the first stop—the Coconino SS in Arizona—for more observations. Except for one blown tire on the rocky back roads and one sick boy, the first stop went well, and we continued driving east. Besides the meetings in Washington, I was anxious to see Charles Gilmore's collection of tracks from the Coconino SS on display in the Smithsonian Institution.

When we arrived in Washington, I headed to the Smithsonian. The on-site paleontologists allowed me to study the tracks and make latex rubber molds of a number of them. From these molds, we could make plaster-of-Paris casts for our teaching and research collection. Two other museums on the American east coast housed excellent collections of fossil tracks, and they also allowed me to make latex molds of the specimens. One was the American Museum in New York, and the other, the Peabody Museum at Yale University. The Peabody collection was largely the work of a prominent nineteenth-century paleontologist, Edward B. Hitchcock.

Leonard Brand and his son, Dennis, collecting fossils
in the Coconino Sandstone, circa 1977.

Finally, I had completed my presentation and the meetings were over, my museum work was done, and we had visited some relatives. We headed west across the northern plains for the Black Hills and a nose-to-nose visit

with George Washington. If you visit the presidents carved in the side of
Mount Rushmore, you can drive just around the corner from the parking
lot and find a place where you can have your picture taken looking right
into Washington's face, with the proper size relationship to make it look
like a face-to-face conference.

The next stop was Bruneau Dunes State Park in southern Idaho. This
field of large sand dunes offered great opportunities to observe lizard tracks
on the sand. We set up camp for the night, and my plan was to get up early
in the morning to study tracks before they were damaged by the wind.
While it was a good plan, we woke up hearing a driving rain on the van
roof, and it was evident my research was finished for this trip. We broke
camp and headed for a family reunion farther north in the beautiful Idaho
mountains—and then the trip home.

Kim, wife of Leonard Brand, and Leonard's son, Dennis, "face to face" with George Washington
at Mount Rushmore in South Dakota, circa 1977.

My paper on the experimental study of tracks was published with the other symposium papers in the European geology journal *Palaeogeography, Palaeoclimatology, Palaeoecology*. Some months later, to my surprise, the paper was chosen for republication in a volume entitled *Benchmark Papers in Geology*. Careful work can pay off, even if it challenges a well-entrenched theory.

My success with that paper didn't mean the work was done and the puzzles all solved. If you found someone's footprints in the desert sand and followed them until the tracks suddenly ended, with no apparent explanation for their ending, what would you think? Trackways just like that can be found in the Coconino SS. Another puzzle was the common occurrence of vertebrate fossil trackways that showed animals walking sideways along the fossilized dune faces, while all their toe marks pointed straight up the dune. In other words, the animal was pointed uphill, but it was actually moving sideways, at almost a right angle to the direction its toes were pointed. To picture this, try running down the road with both feet pointed sideways to your left. On second thought, don't!

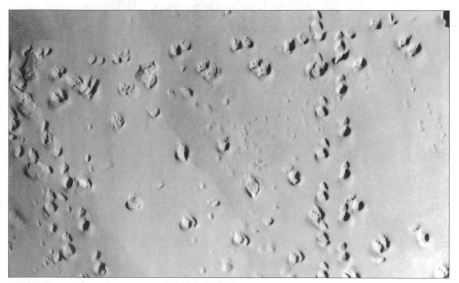

Fossil trackways in the Coconino Sandstone.
Some of them are drifting sideways.

After finding a number of fossil trackways in the Coconino SS that showed sideways movement or abrupt beginnings or endings, I realized another paper was needed. The most striking example was a trackway in a flagstone quarry near Ash Fork, Arizona. The animal had moved sideways along the smooth sand surface, and then the trackway disappeared. About a foot and a half higher, the trackway reappeared and continued sideways in the same direction as before. These were four-footed animals without any wings, so how could their tracks disappear and reappear like that? No change could be noted in the sand that could explain the odd trackways. If the creatures were walking on desert sand, I cannot think of a way to explain those trackways, and no one has been able to give me an explanation. However, if the animals were underwater, the explanation is obvious. They walked on the bottom, then swam up into the water, then swam down and continued walking.

If they were underwater, this also offered a possible explanation for the sideways imprints of the trackways. If the creatures were trying to walk up the underwater sand slope, the main water current would be moving toward them but above their heads. Then gentle lateral currents could possibly push them sideways as they tried to walk up the slope. This called for some more experiments.

In the lab, we prepared a sand surface in a long, aquarium-like tank called a *flume*. A pump moved the water from one end of the flume to the other. A student spent many hours watching salamanders and documenting their movements with a video camera. Salamanders in the flume sometimes walked against the current and made normal trackways. However, if they tried to walk at right angles to the water movement, the current carried them sideways as they tried, in typical plodding salamander fashion, to move forward. The result was a series of footfalls just like the sideways fossil trackways. The video camera recorded this action for detailed, step-by-step analysis.

I wrote up this work in a paper for the journal *Geology*, a prestigious research journal published by the Geological Society of America. The journal editors sent the paper to three reviewers, and I waited with some apprehension for their decision. The manuscript passed the critical eye of reviewers and was published. Not all geologists liked the implications of my conclusions, being still convinced the Coconino SS is a desert sand deposit. Two scientists wrote comments on the paper, trying to show how the tracks could be made on desert sand rather than underwater. These comments the journal sent to me so I could reply, and their comments and my reply were published together. It was not hard to explain why their explanations would not work and that the only feasible interpretation seemed to be animals walking completely underwater. Of course, sometimes ponds are present in the desert, but the fossil tracks are not on the type of sediment that would be expected in such ponds. It seems these fossils were indeed made underwater, maybe even in the great Flood.

Thanksgiving dinner on the Suburban tailgate, 1998.

I took one research trip to the Coconino SS during Thanksgiving vacation in 1998. While I was taking a series of geology classes, a graduate student and I, with my son and a friend along for the ride, made our way to the Route 66 town of Seligman, Arizona. We checked in at the little registration stand maintained by the Navajo Nation, which owns part of the land, and made our way back into the hills. A couple of abandoned sandstone quarries provided ready access to the evidence we sought for our sedimentology class project. Found here were especially fine specimens of fossil trackways and sandstone sedimentary features.

After a day's work, we set up our tents at a KOA campground beside the railroad. That was a mistake! The trains rumbled through all night, and when they weren't keeping us awake, the cold weather was doing the job. In the morning, we changed our minds about saving money with tent camping and moved into a motel in Seligman.

That day at the quarry, we gathered around the tailgate of the Chevrolet Suburban, making sandwiches with cheese, slices of cucumber, vegetarian meat, and other delicacies. One of the group remembered an important detail the rest of us had forgotten: "This is Thanksgiving! And here we are having Thanksgiving dinner on the Suburban tailgate." Memories are made in all kinds of strange places.

Plodding salamanders came through with helpful data, in spite of their slow habits of life. But a sandstone has other features besides fossil trackways that need explaining if the hypothesis of underwater deposition is going to be convincing to many geologists. For example, were the ancient animals that made these tracks reptiles or amphibians? In my lab, many salamanders—that no doubt would rather have been relaxing in a mountain pond—were encouraged to walk on dry sand, wet sand, level sand, level mud, sloping mud, and so on. Tracks on level mud show the most detail and are shaped like the feet of the animal that made them. Tracks on any kind of sloping sand don't have all the information needed to indicate whether they were made by amphibians or by reptiles, so we are still left with unanswered questions about which creatures made these fossil tracks, and those questions will probably remain unanswered. Science does that to us sometimes. The evidence does indicate that it is not legitimate to claim that we know the animals were reptiles and thus they must have been in a desert. That is still an open question.

(4)

DID HUMANS WALK WITH DINOSAURS?

n 1970, a man named Clifford Burdick brought some limestone slabs with fossil footprints to Loma Linda University for my colleagues and me to evaluate. One of the fossil footprints was of a giant human, and the other of a large lion. What phenomenal specimens! The most amazing thing to me was that these were from limestone in the Cretaceous Glen Rose Formation, famous for its dinosaur trackways along the Paluxy River in Texas.

According to accepted geological understanding of earth history, humans did not evolve until about sixty million years after dinosaurs went extinct. In addition, fossil cats don't appear in the rocks until long after the disappearance of the dinosaurs. Would Burdick's fossil tracks disprove the whole evolution theory?

These specimens are part of a story that has been around since the early 1900s of human and dinosaur tracks appearing together in the limestone bed of the Paluxy River. We now had some actual specimens to examine.

Clifford Burdick was a most pleasant gentleman, who had a history of being eager to disprove evolution. We had some nagging questions about his scientific work. His fossil tracks came with official-looking documents—affidavits of authenticity—signed by some impressive-sounding persons and assuring us the fossils were genuine and had been quarried from limestone near Glen Rose, Texas. They were very old documents, dating from the 1930s. Never having seen such affidavits of authenticity, we wondered what they really meant. Did they mean anything at all? Burdick didn't have any affidavits assuring us of the authenticity of the affidavits of authenticity. How far does one go with this kind of thing? One of our biology professors, Berney Neufeld, decided to take on the project.

The footprints in limestone that Burdick had brought to us looked, on the surface, genuine enough. But we needed to know what was below the surface. If the limestone had any horizontal layering or other patterns in it, the patterns should be pushed downward where the ancient feet sank into the lime mud. If the prints had been made by human hands instead of feet—in other words, if they were carved—any layering in the limestone would not follow the shape of the footprint.

The first challenge was to convince Burdick to let us cut his treasured fossils in half. I said to Art Chadwick and Berney Neufeld, "These are Clifford's only claim to fame, and we want to cut them in two!" To our amazement and delight, Burdick agreed to put the fossils through our rock saw. The fossils would never be the same after that, but it seemed to be the only way to know if they were genuine.

We were so eager to test the genuineness of the fossils because, if we could show that humans and big cats and dinosaurs were walking together in the Texas mud, we would have made an extraordinary scientific find. It would repudiate a significant part of the accepted scientific understanding of the evolution of life. But extraordinary claims require extraordinary evidence to support them. The more dramatic the claim, the more careful we must be in examining the evidence. Otherwise, we risk looking foolish and discredited. God is not honored by careless work that doesn't stand up under careful scrutiny.

This is what was at stake: if we could demonstrate that humans and dinosaurs took a walk together long ago, that would be a powerful statement that humans and dinosaurs were not separated by sixty million years of evolutionary time but lived together. On the other hand, if we made the claim of dinosaurs and humans walking together and someone could demonstrate that those human footprints were fakes, it would be an equally powerful destruction of Christian credibility.

The rock saw made its slow but steady way through the prized fossils. Our anticipation was finally rewarded by a view of the interior of the limestone. The interior structure below the human print was inconclusive. The limestone was too homogenous (lacking in distinct layers) to show clearly whether the lime mud had been pushed down by a giant foot. The cat track was more interesting. Some layering was visible in the limestone, and it was not disturbed by any foot pushing down into the mud. The limestone's internal structures were cut at the edge of the track, as would be expected if the impression had been carved.

We concluded that the cat track was a fake. Consequently, we had to consider the possibility the human print was also a fake. We puzzled over why anyone would carve a large cat print or human footprint into this limestone.

Fossil human track from the Paluxy River, Texas. This fake track was apparently carved. The line across the track shows where we sawed it in two.

The explanation came sometime later from an old newspaper report. During the Depression years, some Texans realized there might be a market for large fossilized human footprints to sell to people who were visiting the Paluxy River area to see the famous human and dinosaur tracks. Since just about everyone then was in need of more income, they had incentive for carving accurate human tracks, and apparently cat tracks as well. The sculptors knew that if these prints were to look as though they were from the time of the Flood, the carved footprints would seem more authentic if they were of giant size.

Claims had lived on through the decades after the Depression that fossilized trackways of large humans were present in the limestone, exposed in the bed of the Paluxy River. It didn't seem likely that anyone would go to the trouble of carving a series of tracks right in the river bed, so this called for us to take a trip to Texas to check out the claims.

A fake track that was carved out of limestone. This "cat" track shows
several lines where we sawed through it to see the inside.

The Paluxy River is at its lowest water level in late summer. So in August of 1970, Berney Neufeld, Art Chadwick, and I, along with one of our graduate students, headed east to mid-Texas in my trusty Chevrolet Nova to carry out Berney's research plan.

Arriving at the Paluxy River, we found some beautiful, deeply impressed dinosaur tracks that could be seen across the flat riverbed, not far from the trackway that some had claimed was human. The water across this large section of the river was only about ten inches deep, so we decided it would be feasible to use sandbags and create a dry area of about forty by twenty feet. We would use a pump to drain the water from this enclosure, and the tracks could then be cleared and dried for study.

In the nearby town, we learned that pumps were not readily available for rent, but we finally found one pump that we thought could do the job.

We also needed to replenish our food supply, and a visit to the local supermarket brought an unexpected surprise unrelated to dinosaurs. I wasn't unusually naïve in those days, and on an intellectual level, I understood that parts of the culture in the American south were different from the places where I had spent my life. But on an emotional level, I was quite unprepared for what I saw.

Against one wall of the grocery store was a drinking fountain—the type with the fountain on top of a water cooler. After a good drink, I looked up and noticed a sign on the wall in front of me. The sign had one word: "Colored." The sign was puzzling to me. What could that word *colored* mean? The water was just plain water—not colored at all. The word didn't fit into any concept I could associate with a drinking fountain. Then I noticed, a few feet away, an identical drinking fountain with its own sign that said "White." Then it all became clear, and the absurdity of it struck me like a slap in the face. I had committed the serious error of drinking from the wrong fountain—a fountain devoted to keeping one race separate from another. The dinosaurs might be gone, I thought, but humans still had some things to learn.

Back at the Paluxy, with our load of sand, burlap bags, and a pump, we set to work. We filled the bags with sand and put them in place to form a watertight dam around the section of riverbed with the trackways. Then the pump began its work of removing the water. It worked well for a short time and then quit. We worked over that pump until we realized we were not going to be able to fix it. This was a blow to our plans. We had only a few days in Texas, the pump was out of commission, and no other pumps seemed available in town. We sat there, discouraged, wondering what to do.

Then Art went to work. He found a small bucket and began bailing water from our enclosure. Art has a reputation for going all out when he does something, but I thought this was too much. So much water needed to be removed that surely it would take days to bail it all out with that bucket. One of the others in our group took a photo of me pointing at Art and laughing—but Art had the last laugh. Before long, I noticed the water level going down and began helping to bail instead of laughing. Before the afternoon was gone, the water was all on the other side of the sandbags, and the trackways were ready for our examination.

We could see clear, deep, three-toed dinosaur tracks, and in another part of the enclosure were the famous human tracks. These were elongated tracks, which might be what a human would make as they walked and slipped through the mud. These tracks were not deep and clear like the others but were shallow depressions. They were intriguing, but something about the tracks bothered us. The shape might have been what humans could make, and it could have been a big person, but why weren't there any toe marks or other details, as might be expected?

As the sun moved across the sky, making us wish for air conditioning, the changes in the lighting on our study plot made different features of the tracks more evident. We could see that the tracks were not just elongated grooves, but some prints showed evidence of additional toes in the same positions as the three-toed dinosaur tracks. It became more and more obvious that this was the track of another three-toed dinosaur that had been badly eroded. All that was left was a series of these shallow, elongated grooves, showing the middle toe, with only an occasional remnant of the side toes. The animal may have been slipping in the mud, making the tracks more elongated than expected. Careful observation had kept us from making an unfortunate mistake. We also had noted that the limestone in this area did not seem to match the details of the limestone containing Burdick's giant human track. That track was evidently carved in a limestone slab from somewhere else.

The trusty Nova brought us swiftly back to Loma Linda, and Berney Neufeld published an article in the journal *Origins* that described our findings. Other creationists independently came to similar conclusions, and many creationists abandoned the theory of human and dinosaur tracks appearing together at the Paluxy River.

What had we actually accomplished? We had not disproven or undermined the biblical flood or some other biblical belief. I have not found the terms *Cretaceous* or *Paluxy*, or even *dinosaur*, in my Bible. The idea that humans and dinosaurs walked together in Texas is purely a human theory. We did cut Clifford Burdick's dream fossils in two, but we didn't damage the Bible. The biblical creation account indicates that humans were on the earth from the original creation and thus must have lived during the time when dinosaurs were becoming fossils. But that doesn't tell us they were both in Texas at the same time.

The lack of human fossils in much of the fossil record indicates that for some reason, humans did not live in the areas where fossils were being formed during those times. We were not present back then to observe what happened, so we don't know the reasons. What we do know is that human beings were apparently not in Texas walking with the dinosaurs. To this day, at least one creationist website continues to insist that humans did walk with dinosaurs in Texas, and if you look closely at the site's photos of a certain human track and cat track in a slab of limestone, you will see the lines made by our rock saw many years ago!

$$\widehat{5}$$

THE ARGUMENT, THE WINDSTORM, AND THE TURTLE HUNT

U p in southwestern Wyoming, in the Bridger Formation, there are fossil turtles all over the place. Why don't you come up and study them?"

My geologist friend Paul Buchheim tried for several years to interest me in the Bridger Formation. But the name "Bridger Formation" was just a set of unfamiliar words that didn't catch my imagination at the time. I also couldn't see my way clear to spending weeks up there away from my wife and young children. How could I forgo that hour each night at the children's bedtime, talking about their day, reading or telling stories, singing songs, praying to God, and singing them to sleep? If I neglected those experiences, they would not come back later.

Then, in the late summer of 1989, I went with other scholars to Rock Springs, Wyoming, for a conference on origins, including a field trip in the Bridger Formation. One evening, I listened carefully as three friends were arguing about how the Eocene Bridger Formation and the closely related Green River Formation could relate to the biblical global flood. Paleontologist Lee Spencer and geologist Elaine Kennedy argued that the sequence of vertebrate fossils in the Bridger Formation and other fluvial (deposited by flowing water) rock formations could be explained only if they were deposited during the Flood. Paul Buchheim, who had studied the Green River Formation (GRF) for years, was convinced the GRF must have formed after the Flood, because its lake sediments (*lacustrine*—deposited in the standing water of a lake) and fossils showed much evidence of an established ecology, instead of being washed in by a great flood. The middle of the lake had large fossil fish, while the sediments near shore contained many juvenile fish, cattails, fly larvae, and other creatures that would live near the shore. This was an interesting conflict of interpretations because the Bridger Formation and the GRF formed at the same time. The GRF accumulated in ancient Lake Gosiute and the Bridger in the flood plain beside the lake. Since they formed at the same time, they both had to form during—or both after—the global Flood. Or did they fit the Flood story at all?

I listened to the conversation and decided there was reason to take an interest in the Bridger Formation after all—to try to solve this puzzle. In addition, my wife had begun working summers as camp nurse at the Pine Springs Ranch summer camp, so our children were in camp all summer. Each week of the summer, they were engrossed in horsemanship, rock climbing, water skiing, or swimming. This meant my family was well cared for in the summer, so the Wyoming fossil turtles gained a higher place in my interest.

At a lunch at the end of the Rock Springs conference, a group of us decided to go back to the Bridger Formation for a couple more days of exploration. As we savored our pizza, it was raining hard. This was not good, because the Bridger Formation contains a lot of clay, and driving or walking on wet clay is like walking on greased slime—with each step, another half inch of the gooey clay sticks to your boots.

The rain finally stopped, so we took our chances and headed for the Bridger at the foot of Black Mountain. At one especially steep hill, it took us more than an hour to take four vehicles up the rugged, slippery trail. Lee's four-wheel-drive pickup slipped and slid up the hill, dropping bags of plaster of Paris and other collecting supplies as it fought its way to the top of the slope. We camped on a flat bench along the base of the mountain. It was a pleasant setting, close to many fossils, but it faced west, and there was nothing between us and the occasional fierce Wyoming winds except a few barbed-wire fences.

We spent the daytime hours finding fossil turtles, mammal teeth, garfish scales and vertebrae, and crocodile teeth and bones. The most abundant were the turtle shells, and they really were all over the place. This would end up being the site of my research for the next few summers. I wondered, *Would this research yield meaningful results and published papers?* Some of us in my field love the opportunity to challenge the unknown and to solve fascinating puzzles. For me, there is also the reward of seeking a better understanding of the relationship between the rocks and the Book—the Bible.

That night, we prepared for sleep in our tents overlooking the valley. During the night, the weather determined to rival Polecat Bench with winds that will destroy all but the most stubborn tents. It seemed the wind was intent on discouraging us from our turtle hunt. However, it underestimated our determination. We didn't give up; we began planning the research trip for the following summer.

The next summer, Paul Buchheim and his family, along with two students and me, headed north toward Wyoming. We left home about four o'clock in the morning with two field vehicles. I drove the university Suburban, pulling Paul's camping trailer.

In the next few years, we would learn each significant twist and turn of that long road from Loma Linda to southwest Wyoming. The environment and culture along each part of the road north has its own character. From San Bernardino to Barstow, Interstate 15 follows historic old US Highway 66—the famous two-lane highway from Chicago to Santa Monica. In the years before the interstate highways, many adventuresome people traveled Route 66 in search of their dreams.

At Barstow, the freeway splits because of that magnificent barrier to travel, the Grand Canyon. Interstate 40 follows Route 66, going south of the Grand Canyon. Interstate 15 continues east and north, winding its way between the desert hills to Baker, a bleak cluster of service stations and restaurants. Baker appropriately proclaims itself "The Gateway to Death Valley."

Beyond Baker is a forty-mile stretch with a couple of passes through the desert mountains, with a thin scatter of unimpressive little bushes, searching for a resting place in Nevada. At the bottom of the pass, we enter Nevada, where every service station and hotel has slot machines and other gambling devices seeking to separate us from our money. We would make our way along the highway through Las Vegas, with its line of casinos, as fast as possible. Then, after a short run through the corner of Arizona, we finally arrived in the fascinating scenery of Utah. And since the elevation is higher, it is also a rest from the worst of the desert heat.

The line of mountains along scenic Interstate 15 guided us through central Utah to Salt Lake City, resting beneath extensive, fascinating platforms that are the ancient shorelines of Lake Bonneville, which once filled all the valleys in southwest Utah. Some of the higher-priced housing occupies the benches that compose these old shorelines. If Lake Bonneville filled up again, Salt Lake City and many other places would simply disappear underwater. The ancient past was very different from the world we know now.

In Salt Lake City, we turned east again and climbed along the old Mormon Trail through a long canyon that winds its way up into Wyoming, into new research adventures awaiting us there. On this trip, with the trailer slowing us down, we arrived at the camp on the hill above Fossil Butte National Monument about midnight.

The camp was situated on a high ridge in a grove of small pine trees, overlooking a series of valleys and ridges stretching west into northern Utah. We shared the grove with deer, moose, chipmunks, and the occasional porcupine. My tent site on the north side of the ridge looked across a broad valley to the next ridge. Outside the tent, my camp chair was an inspirational setting for morning devotionals. The scene from there was also a reminder of some fascinating history, as a branch of the Oregon Trail traversed the distant ridge on its way west. How many long-ago travelers passed that way in search of their dreams? Many traveled there, and some died there, before the discovery of penicillin and SUVs.

The group of paleontologists and students quarrying fossils
in the Bridger Formation, at Black Mountain, Wyoming.

In the few weeks available that summer, I helped Paul at first with his work in the GRF, and then the whole crew came to the Bridger Formation for reconnaissance work, finding the best locations for research to begin the following summer. We first went to Butcher Knife Draw (one has to wonder about the history of names like this) and surveyed the fossil content there in the greenish sediments, formed mostly of clay, with sandstones above the clay unit. The fossils were much like those at Black Mountain. Along with the plentiful turtles, there were thin layers that held small-mammal teeth and jaws, fish vertebrae, crocodile bones, and other small fossils—an assemblage that paleontologists call microvertebrates. We spent time doing what vertebrate paleontologists often do, crawling on hands and knees with nose close to the ground to find little fossil treasures among the dirt and pebbles.

Then it was back to the site at Black Mountain to compare the two areas. The fossils at Black Mountain are also in a greenish clay unit, with extensive turtle-rich surfaces. If you find a turtle that is mostly still buried, with just a small part exposed at the surface, you can excavate it and have a complete turtle shell. But often the sediment covering the turtles had already been eroded away, leaving a pile of disarticulated turtle bones. With patience and stubborn persistence, you can put the shell together like a puzzle. I admit that it was usually students who did that part. The turtles were almost all pond or river turtles, from about six inches to a foot and a half in size across the shell.

Paleontologist and student finding small mammal
fossils in the Bridger Formation.

Paleontologists have been visiting the Bridger Formation and collecting fossils since the transcontinental railroad, which passed through the formation, was completed in 1869. A "fossil feud" between rival paleontologists Edward Drinker Cope and Othniel Marsh began here in the Bridger. They each had a crew in the western US collecting fossils, which they named in quickly written papers—rushed out sometimes too quickly— for publication. Their goal was to name as many fossil animal species as possible before their rival did, to become more famous. They did *some* good work, but they also created confusion in the paleontology literature, which later scientists had to unravel. Cope, in his haste, once published a paper showing a fossil reptile's head on the wrong end of the skeleton! That, too, can make a man famous.

We chose to focus on the turtles for a practical reason. In successive rock layers, one above the other, the mammal fossils change, so for the past century and a quarter, the paleontologists have been most interested in collecting fossil mammals for their research on mammal evolution. The fossil turtles don't change much through the layers, so the collectors have ignored the turtles.

5.3 A fossil turtle from the Bridger Formation in Wyoming.

Most of the fossil mammals at the rock surface have been collected, but because scientists had ignored the turtles, we could find enough of them to make trustworthy comparisons of how many ancient turtles there are in each area. Since our research required this type of quantitative information, turtles were the logical research animal for us. Our research would be on the *taphonomy* of turtles. Taphonomy is basically the study of dead and rotting things. A more delicate definition is the study of the processes from death to fossilization of organisms. The goal is to determine how and why some creatures or plants were fossilized and some others were not, and what were the conditions and the time frame of the fossilization process.

You can do some taphonomy research yourself. If you see a fresh dead cat on the road, kick it into the ditch. Then come back every day and take notes on what is happening: when different kinds of insects come to feed or lay eggs, how long it takes for the tissue to disappear and the skeleton to fall apart—fun observations like that. Such data can help us understand why fossils are in the condition they are. For one example, let's say you are digging in the rocks and find a piece of fossil bone, all by itself, that was broken before it was buried. There is always a reason why it is broken and separated from the rest of the skeleton. Taphonomy is the search for such answers.

The campsite at Cedar Mountain in Wyoming.

We found a great spot for a campsite that became our home for a number of summers. In a little valley mostly surrounded by small hills was a group of scattered juniper trees along one side. Beyond these hills rose Cedar Mountain, so this site came to be called our Cedar Mountain camp. The hills surrounding the valley were composed primarily of sandstone. That is an important detail because when it rained, our camp would not be a quagmire of sticky clay. It was just far enough from the dirt "road" to be somewhat private. At the edge of the camp was a narrow opening between sandstone outcroppings, just the right spot for a portable toilet with a tarp to cover the entrance. Scattered among the junipers were delightful spots for tents.

The surrounding hills provided some shelter, but that didn't help much against the Wyoming wind. One night, the wind began to blow fiercely. My little pup tent, which had often been my shelter on camping trips since junior high, didn't seem to be holding up well. From inside the tent, I held down the corners that came loose and waited for morning. The wind had ripped out the canvas tent-peg loops on each corner of the tent. I faced the fact that my old friend had reached its last season and drove the tent pegs through the corners of the tent. The next summer I would require a stronger tent.

One other thing I learned that summer—don't pitch your tent close to the big red ant hills so common in Wyoming.

(6)

HEADLESS TURTLES AND SUBURBAN SURPRISES

No motivator is quite as effective for getting a research project in gear as a graduate student eager to start on his thesis research. In 1991, one such student, whom I'll call Jim, was ready to get going. So, we began planning a trip to Black Mountain in Wyoming.

I had a dream of something that would greatly facilitate fieldwork—a trailer built as a life support system. We could have bought a self-contained camping trailer, but they are too big and fragile for the rugged country and off-road trails in Wyoming. I had seen a custom-built trailer used by a youth organization, and their concept could be modified for our purpose.

A trailer company took my plans and built the chassis and metal frame. Then we took it home and built in the kitchen and storage spaces. When I took it back to the trailer builder for the external covering, our tight budget became an advantage. They gave me their estimate of the cost for the covering, and I said, "We can't afford that, so we will cover it with plywood and fiberglass." They were not happy, because the trailer frame already had their company name on it. No doubt, they had visions of an ugly trailer with their brand attached!

The trailer builders sharpened their pencils and came back with a substantially revised estimate that was within our budget. We picked up the completed project, and the "chuck wagon" has been a unique and treasured research aid since then. It is compact and durable enough to go wherever our four-wheel-drive vehicles can go. One side is an RV-style kitchen, with propane range and refrigerator, and the other side is storage space. A long compartment opening to the back carries two folding tables, chairs, shovels, and other supplies. Water from the forty-gallon tank goes to the kitchen sink, passing through a filter for safety. We also included a small wooden box that contains another RV water pump and filter and a long cord to plug into the car power outlet. That little box served us well in the field when the only water source was a cattle-watering trough fed by a spring.

Breakfast for the paleontologists at the chuckwagon.

As I was leaving home at four o'clock in the morning for that summer's trip, I hurriedly opened the front door of my house and immediately came face to face with a large skunk. I quickly and respectfully stepped back, expecting the worst. Fortunately, he retreated as fast as I did.

The long drive to Wyoming landed us again at the base of Black Mountain. We camped on the same flat from which we were almost blown away two summers earlier. It was not as elegant as the Cedar Mountain camp, but it was only yards from the edge of our research site. Black Mountain loomed on one side of the twenty acres of more-or-less horizontal, turtle-rich mudstone exposure.

Many questions ran through my mind that were motivating this research. Other Bridger researchers thought the turtles had lived in localized ponds, lakes, and marshes and died there over eons of time. Were they right? Or are the fossils part of more geographically extensive turtle deposits? How long did it take to form these fossil assemblages? Were the turtles living where they died, or were they transported there from somewhere else? How catastrophic were the processes forming the Bridger sediments and fossils, and how did all of this relate to the Flood?

Jim and I spent the first afternoon locating turtles and marking them with little plastic flags. Some scattered turtle-shell bones were lying around, but we only marked bone groups that had enough bones to indicate a turtle. By the time we had used up almost all of our four hundred flags, I was thinking that this was not a local population of turtles in a pond. Jim cautiously asked, "Could this have been formed by a catastrophe?" We needed much more evidence to answer that question.

Now that we knew the full extent of the fossil deposit, we could refine our research strategy. To document just how many turtles existed and where they were located, we used surveying methods to make a detailed map of the twenty acres and the bordering hills—and the locations of all turtles. These specimens were mostly on the surface, but what were they like before they eroded out of the mudstone? To answer that question, we chose a quarry site of several square meters and began a careful excavation. A map of the quarry was also needed, with the location of all bones pinpointed on the map. The task was made easier by the fact that the turtle bones were not vertically scattered through the mudstone but were essentially all on one level.

Vertebrate fossils are protected by law, but we had a permit from the

Bureau of Land Management that allowed us to collect the needed fossils and maintain them at the university. We collected many bones for detailed study back in the lab to reveal the stories behind them.

Among the questions we wished to answer with our field study were the following: Were the bones weathered from much time lying in the sun before they were buried? And were the edges abraded from being transported by water and bounced against rocks?

It turned out the bones were not weathered and did not show evidence of abrasion. Evidently, they had not spent much time weathering in the sun, and they weren't abraded by water transport. A few pieces of the story were emerging, but why were we finding so many turtle shells and no skulls and only a few limb bones? A study of modern turtles provided a helpful answer.

Leonard Brand's daughter, Jenelle, on horseback
at Pine Springs Ranch summer camp.

When turtles die, the first part that comes loose from the animal is the head, and that happens in about a week. Not long afterward, the limbs separate from the body. The shell is the most durable, lasting up to five months in water. Our fossil turtles were all in about the same stage of decay, which means they were all killed at the same time. Then they were buried after their heads fell off and most limbs came loose but before the shells disarticulated. That tells us they were all buried within a few weeks to a few months after death. The joke in camp for the next few years was that one day we would find in the rocks a big pile of fossil turtle skulls. So far, we haven't found the turtle skull bonanza.

Paul Buchheim and his sedimentology crew spent time with us, beginning their study of the sediments that contain the turtles. Their work included what geologists call "measuring a section." A geological section is a stack of rock layers. Measuring a section means measuring how thick each layer is, describing the rocks in a field book, and collecting rock samples for lab study to determine exactly what kind of rock it is.

Fossils help indicate the paleoenvironment (ancient environment), but they are not enough. When paleontologists and geologists work together, they can generate a better set of evidences to unravel the secrets of ancient history. Of course, a fringe benefit is a camp with three professors and half a dozen students, where life is never dull. Dr. Paul was a good sport and fun to tease. He could also give some back!

Jim and I wanted to find evidence in these rocks to give clues about the paleoenvironment in which the rocks formed and how the rocks were deposited. Did the sediments accumulate in a lake, or were they deposited in a river valley, carried there by the flooding river?

Research in southwest Wyoming is not complete without a weekend of rest amid the grandeur of the Wind River Range. Its long ridge of rugged granite peaks, some more than 14,000 feet in elevation, starts at South Pass and points northwest, like a long finger, toward the Teton Range. South Pass was God's gift to the pioneers in their wagon trains. It's the only place where a gently sloping pass allowed the Oregon Trail to cross the continental divide without negotiating jagged mountain terrain. On this trip, we chose Green River Lakes in the north end of the Wind River Range for a resting place. The Green River begins in high mountain valleys and flows north through the Green River Lakes, before changing its mind and making a wide turn, heading south to the Colorado River in Utah.

Leonard Brand at a study site in the Bridger Formation, Wyoming.

On Thursday, the day before our planned trip, we collected some rock samples in a precarious location. Along its western edge, the Bridger Formation ends in a long, meandering, steep bluff about a thousand feet high. We drove across the plateau to the top of the bluff. Our collecting site was at the bottom, and no road led down from the bluff in this area. Did we really want to carry five-gallon buckets of rocks up this hill? One possible route down followed a natural gas pipeline that had been buried a few years before. Bulldozers had gone directly down the crest of a steep ridge into the valley. From a distance, it looked as if we could drive down this bulldozer route. Then, as I drove to the top of the bluff, I had doubts, since we could not see over the bluff's top to the "road" below. We got out, walked down the ridge, and decided our vehicle could manage, so we drove over the edge and down the bluff. Later, with full buckets loaded, we backed farther down the hill and then roared forward, confident the Suburban would get us up the precipitous ridge with its steep slopes falling away on either side of us. In spite of a little wheel-spinning on some wet places, we made it to the top without incident.

After a two-hour drive on Friday afternoon, we reached our favorite campground in the pine trees along placid Green River Lake. We stepped out of the Suburban and immediately jumped back in, pursued by swarms of hungry mosquitoes. After exchanging short pants and short-sleeved shirts for better protection, we tried again. The next task was to back the chuck wagon and Suburban into a campsite. This should have been easy, but at that moment, the Suburban did not respond to my pressure on the accelerator. The engine roared, but nothing happened, except that the vehicle tried to coast back downhill. No connection seemed evident between the engine and the wheels.

With the input of a Chevrolet repairman who happened to be staying nearby, we determined that our transmission was suddenly nonfunctional. With the help of kind neighbors, we pushed our vehicles into place for the weekend. Now, how would we get help out here in the mountain wilds, with the nearest telephone forty miles away?

The camp host was a kind man, and we came to appreciate him more as the weekend progressed. Saturday night, he used his National Forest Service radio to reach a friend, the local sheriff. The sheriff called the Chevrolet dealer in Rock Springs, where our transmission had been overhauled two weeks earlier, and arranged for a tow truck to make the two-hour trip to pick us up. The truck could not come until Monday, so we settled in for a pleasant long weekend of hiking amid the lakes and magnificent scenery and spotting an occasional moose.

I had plenty of time to ponder our situation and wonder why the transmission had given out just as we reached camp and not sometime earlier. It appeared that Someone was watching over us. What would have happened had the transmission blown the day before, while it was straining to get us up that steep bluff? I didn't dwell on that but was thankful to God for a safe ride.

We were able to return to Black Mountain with a fixed transmission. By the end of the trip, our map was finally finished, and the rock samples were mailed back to Loma Linda, along with many turtle bones for analysis in the lab. Another field excursion was finished. We didn't yet know the answers to our biggest questions, but our primary objective for this summer was accomplished—Jim had the material for his thesis.

7

RETURN TO CEDAR MOUNTAIN

Would our Suburban fail us again? That question often entered our minds as we spent time in the wilderness, where our vehicle was our lifeline. We always carried a tire-repair kit and a battery-powered tire pump, but would that be enough?

This year, 1992, our research team camped at our Cedar Mountain camp and continued pondering the headless fossil turtles. We knew how many turtles were at Black Mountain, and even though it was many more than we expected, we still had to ask how we could know whether it was a dense local concentration of turtles or some other phenomenon that we had uncovered.

To find the answer, we had to keep following that greenish mudstone layer as far as we could. My colleague Tom Goodwin and I wondered if this was a practical plan because as soon as we followed the green layer around the corner from last year's study area, it became just a ledge partway up the steep, rugged eastern face of Black Mountain. After a few hikes along the mountain face, we understood why this side of the mountain is called Devil's Playground.

To make matters worse, the entire mountain had been designated by the Bureau of Land Management (BLM) as a Wilderness Study Area. That meant the agency was studying whether it should be designated a Wilderness Area, and immediately the same rules as for a Wilderness Area would apply. To establish the area as a Wilderness Area would take an act of Congress, but the agency can simply name it a Wilderness Study Area without approval from anyone. The local hunters would drive their all-terrain vehicles anywhere on the mountain, but we couldn't risk losing our research permits, so we would have to park at the study area boundary and walk a mile to the base of the mountain before climbing all the way up to the layers containing turtles.

The hillside at Devil's Playground. The horizontal lines are limestones, some of which have abundant fossil turtles.

During these climbs, we learned that there are three layers of interest in the rock layers. Near the bottom is a limestone, capped by a greenish mudstone, with many turtles. We called it the lower turtle layer. About thirty meters of slipping and sliding up the steep mudstone above it is another limestone, capped by yet another mudstone, with only an occasional turtle. Because of the color of this limestone, we called it the golden bench limestone. Another forty meters higher is the layer we studied the previous year. We called it the green turtle layer.

This interesting find offered the possibility of answering at least two questions. One question was the one with which we began this season's trip—how far does last year's turtle concentration continue along the green turtle layer? Another intriguing question was why these three layers all seem to be formed of the same sediments, yet two have lots of turtles and the middle one has only a few turtles. And a third question arose: How many hikes would it take, up and down Devil's Playground with backpacks of rock and fossil samples before we would know the answers to the first two questions? It turned out to be a good thing we could not foresee the answer to this third question.

Students quarrying fossil turtles in the Bridger Formation, Wyoming.

We quickly learned one other lesson. While clawing our way up the steep slope, we should not grab onto the small, green succulent bushes because under the soft, inviting-looking foliage were long, wicked thorns!

On our way down the slope each afternoon, we carried a heavy load of rock samples. Through the years, rain had softened the outer layer of the rocky hillside, often soft enough so we could run down the slope as if it were a snowdrift.

Another feature that keeps away boredom in this sagebrush country is the common development of clouds in mid-afternoon that produce a thunder-shower. The desolate mountainside is an eerie place to be amid the rain and lightning, but here and there under the limestone layers are eroded hollow places big enough to shelter a small research crew from the rain. As we worked our way along the mountain face, we kept track of where the nearest shelter was. A group of clouds would begin to grow into a dark, threatening mass. The clouds provided welcome shade, but when the wind started to blow, it was time to head for one of those shelters before the rain descended. The fierce wind and rain would last about twenty minutes, and then we could go back to work. Usually, our tents, back in camp, survived those winds, but not always.

Innocent-looking, fuzzy bushes on
the steep hillsides at Devil's Playground.

One afternoon, Tom Goodwin and I were alone on the slopes of Devil's Playground when the dark mass of clouds built up, and then the wind started. We found a rock shelter, but it wasn't very big. Our plastic ponchos were an adequate cover for our legs and feet, which were longer than the overhanging limestone ledge. That worked for a while until the ledge began to leak. More and more water found its way through cracks in the ledge and down our necks to dampen our enthusiasm. The lightning strikes nearby on the mountain added to our doubts about this situation. People do die from lightning strikes on these hillsides, so it wasn't wise to take chances.

The thorns hiding under the leaves of the soft-looking bush.

We waited for the usual end of the rainstorm, but in time, we began to think this one wasn't going to end anytime soon. Finally, a lightning strike that came a little too close chased us out of our leaking hideout. We decided this was not one of those brief storms and we had better make a run for it. The clay was slippery, and the car was a mile away. We headed out across a long, flat ridge, the best way to move quickly. Another close lightning strike chased Tom off the ridge into a draw, but I kept running along the ridge. We finally met at the bottom of the mountain and made our slippery way to the car. So ended that day's work.

The rainstorms had a unique way of forming. A mass of clouds would form with blue sky around them, and rain poured from the clouds. On one occasion, rain chased Paul and me off that same mountain, and as we ran, we came out of the rain, but we could see and hear it pouring down a few yards from us.

Each day we followed a familiar procedure at Cedar Mountain camp. I got up at six o'clock in the morning for my personal devotion time on some "comfortable" rock seat on the hillside. At seven, I shouted a wake-up call to the others and started the generator to make it difficult for them to go back to sleep. The generator also kept our trailer battery charged and powered the toaster for breakfast. After breakfast, we each made our lunch and put it into the Suburban. When those tasks were finished, we gathered around the table for the group morning devotional, led in turn by one of the group. We left camp between eight o'clock and eight thirty and headed for Black Mountain. At the end of the day on the mountain, after the field books with turtle data and the rock samples were safely packed in our backpacks, we made the pilgrimage back to the Suburban and back to camp for supper and some relaxation.

The procedure was altered each weekend. Our camps did not offer such luxuries as showers or clothes-washing machines. Each Friday, work stopped at noon, and we headed for town. The order of events there began with a trip to the showers at the town recreation center. The camp rule was that everybody took a shower, whether they felt like having one or not! Then after a visit to the post office to pick up mail, the next stop was a laundromat and then the grocery store to restock our chuck wagon. On Sabbath, we attended the Adventist church in town, and our crew sometimes doubled the size of the delightfully loving, Christ-centered congregation. In the afternoon, we had a potluck meal at the church, followed by a trip to sing at a home for old folks, then a walk along the river or a drive to some other location that offered refreshing time amidst God's created wonders.

On one such afternoon, Tom Goodwin and I drove across Cedar Mountain to the top of the precipitous southern side, overlooking the valley between Cedar Mountain and the much larger Uinta Mountains in northern Utah, just a few miles away. From our vantage point, I looked down at a range of small hills called the Bald Range. As I studied it, I suddenly realized something unique about this specific layout of ridges—something different from all the other Bridger badlands. I exclaimed to Tom, "Those ridges are giant ripples!"

Climbing the steep hillsides at Devil's Playground.

The ridges had the shape of giant water-current ripples as if formed at some time in the past by a massive flow of water between Cedar Mountain and the Uinta Mountains, flowing toward the nearby place where the Green River has cut a deep gorge through the Uinta Mountains. Tom was cautious about my on-the-spot geological interpretation, but with more study, he verified that the Bald Range ridges do have intriguing features that deserve formal study. I will probably never have time to follow up on that, and it is another puzzle waiting to be solved.

As we looked down the side of Cedar Mountain, a second surprise of a very different sort was waiting. We could see that along the steep slopes of the mountain, about a fourth of the way down from the top, was a level where occasional springs emerged at the surface and supported clusters of cottonwood trees. Here and there were signs of old beaver ponds, and just below us was an active pond. Walking across the meadow near this pond was a moose. Moose are common in the Uintas but not on Cedar Mountain. It seems that a moose had come across the valley and found this little moose oasis at the beaver pond. We decided that someday we should come back and find our way to the beaver pond.

Back at Devil's Playground, we needed to know the distribution of turtles along the mudstones to answer our research questions. Our impressions of turtle abundance would not be enough. We needed numbers of bones in each 100 square meters of rock surface exposure. We ended up using the hectare as our unit of measure, which is equal to about two and a half acres. We could not count every turtle in many miles of rock layers, so we arbitrarily chose seven study sites along Devil's Playground. If we chose the sites with the most turtles, it would bias our results, so we chose the random study sites on a map before we even saw them.

The turtle-counting procedure was to mark out and measure the size of plots along the mudstone surfaces at these sites, each about fifty meters long and five to twenty meters wide. Then, in each plot, we counted all isolated turtle bones and all turtle bone piles and estimated how many bones were in each pile (ranging from five to a hundred bones). Since we didn't excavate these bone piles to see if each was a complete turtle, we didn't know the absolute numbers of turtles. But we used the number of piles with thirty or more bones, and this gave a standard estimate of turtle numbers that we could compare between sites and between rock layers. We also collected sediment samples at each study site on each of the three mudstone layers.

Why, I wondered to myself, have we been back to this same site on the hillside three times? Why didn't we collect all the data we needed the first time we were here? Are we that disorganized? After more reflection, the answer was clear. The first time at that site we collected the information we thought was important. Then after working at another site, we noticed some new features in the rocks. Had they also been a feature at the first site and we didn't notice? We had to go back and look. It is common to find new things on a second or third or even fourth visit at the same site. That is the nature of research. It is a continual learning process, going back and checking places we have been before.

After a couple of field seasons of this work, we developed a sort of love-hate relationship with Devil's Playground—a wonderful location that yielded abundant data for objective analysis of turtle distributions. The cost was the daily struggle up the mountain and the return with heavy loads of samples. After our initial study of rock samples, Paul Buchheim and his students joined us for a more detailed study of the sediments along our three rock layers. Since Paul had talked me into working in the Bridger Formation, he owed me some good sedimentology analysis of our turtle sites!

8

DON'T LET THE ROCKS GET THE BEST OF YOU

After several years of climbing up and down Devil's Playground, our research team had extracted several fascinating conclusions from its punishing slopes. We knew that the fossil turtles were concentrated in a few mudstone layers, each appearing right above a limestone. Each limestone was formed in a lake. The turtles occurred in the first few meters of mudstone above each limestone. The lower turtle layer and the green turtle layer, with their fine-grained mudstones, had many turtles—up to 200 turtles per hectare. The mudstone above the golden bench limestone had very few turtles, and this could be because it was deposited when water flow over the area was much more rapid.

The Bridger Formation has been divided into five units of area, from bottom to top, called units A to E. Unit B covers the largest geographic area by far, and our research was in Bridger B. Bridger units C to E have been eroded away from most of that area, except for several mountains along the southern part of the formation—Sage Creek Mountain, Hickey Mountain, Cedar Mountain, and Black Mountain. Someone else was studying Bridger C to E.

In 1994, we decided the time had arrived to find the beaver pond on the side of Cedar Mountain. After work, we packed some food and headed for a trail we had located on the map. Some interesting off-road driving took us up the side of the mountain to the pond. We quietly approached the side of the pond and settled ourselves in position, with a large beaver lodge in view. As the sun slid lower in the west and the light dimmed, our patience was rewarded. Several beavers appeared from the lodge, and two large ones came along the bank near us. We wondered whether they were curious about us or just trying to protect their domain, because they stayed in the water within a few yards of us, eating bark from poplar branches and swimming back and forth. We decided we would have to come back at another time for a rerun of this fascinating look into beaver life.

The high concentrations of turtles in the lower turtle layer and the green turtle layer extended across at least eight miles of the Devil's Playground hillside. I wondered whether they went farther. Twenty miles away, at Butcher Knife Draw and along the base of Cedar Mountain, the abundant turtles were also in greenish mudstones. Could there be any connection between these widely separated green mudstones? We began to wonder whether the published literature was wrong in persistently claiming these limestones were formed in discontinuous local water bodies.

Two students and I began to follow a prominent limestone near Cedar Mountain. We followed it from hillside to hillside to the west and north, comparing in each hill the character of the limestone and the fossils just above and below it. This continued for mile after mile, with the limestone forming an extensive flat bench. Eventually, we noticed that wherever we followed this limestone, we could see a turtle-rich green mudstone roughly forty meters above it. At the base of the green mudstone was another limestone, or in places, the limestone changed to a whitish limey mudstone, but it was always a continuous pair—a whitish limey layer capped by a conspicuous green mudstone with lots of turtles.

Was this the same as our green turtle layer at Black Mountain, or a different, local deposit? If it were the same layer, we predicted certain places where we would find it in the valleys between Cedar Mountain and Black Mountain. With anticipation, we shifted the Suburban into four-wheel drive and headed out cross-country.

We found exposures of the green mudstone with turtles right where we predicted they would be. Then we went back to that lower, prominent limestone and followed it to the east, toward Black Mountain. It continued along the edge of the bench until, at Black Mountain, it was obviously our golden bench limestone, about forty meters below the green turtle layer. Another piece of the puzzle was in place! These rock layers were continuous over an extensive area.

Now, with our enthusiasm in high gear, we continued mapping both layers and looking for other layers that could be mapped. This type of mapping of prominent layers, often called *marker beds*, is an important part of paleontology research. Until this mapping is done on an extensive scale, it is not possible to know which fossils in one place are the same age as fossils in another place, in another part of the formation. Ideally, such mapping should be one of the first stages in paleontology and geology research, but in more than a century of research, most of the Bridger Formation had not been mapped. We needed that information, so we continued mapping.

Now that the mapping project was underway, it was mostly a one-person task. That meant that I spent weeks alone—up to two months in some summers. Working alone in the wilderness is not a recommended procedure and is not my preference, but it needed to be done. Otherwise, the mapping could drag on for years.

Questions tumbled around in my mind. *Would most of the limestones continue over a wide area, or would there be many different, local limestone layers?* Of course, this question is one of the important ones I wished to answer, so this was my reason for being there. I was thinking that a more catastrophic process would be likely to produce deposits that cover a large area, rather than local ponds each producing its own local limestone. But a scientist cannot decide ahead of time what the answer should be. If they were mostly local limestones, that would be my answer. If each layer continued over the whole basin, that would be my answer. What would I find?

I felt some tension each time I prepared to leave the safety and comfort of camp for a couple of days alone in the wilderness, taking along five gallons of water, a little food, and a sleeping bag. What would this trip bring? Was it even possible to do what I was attempting to do? If so, why hadn't anyone else done it before in the Bridger Formation, through more than a century of research conducted by geologists and paleontologists?

Another question was stirring in my mind: At the end of the day, would my four-wheel-drive SUV bring me back to camp? The project required many miles of walking and driving on some good off-road trails but also on some trails hardly worthy of the name (a pair of tire tracks, called two-tracks), and cross country, often through terrain rarely visited. Difficult areas needed to be covered on foot. In the evening, would all be well, or would I be stuck in some unexpected washout in the road? At a couple of off-road locations, the rabbits and pronghorn acted as if they had never seen a human or a car before.

But the tension and questions pushed me on. Mapping rock layers had not been my goal in coming to this country, but it was a necessary part of accomplishing the overall purpose of the project.

What were the relationships between rock layers and fossils on the near hillside and the rock layers miles away? Determining these relationships turned out to be one of the more interesting puzzles I have tackled. Picture an irregularly shaped mountain made of horizontal layers of rock. Erosion has removed the rock from around the mountain, so the layers are visible on the edge of the mountain and extend into and through the mountain to the other side. My task was to walk and drive along the visible edge of the layers and draw their location on topographic maps or aerial photographs, and then find the same layers in other locations. In the Bridger Formation Unit B, this meant covering several hundred square miles, keeping track of a dozen rock layers (marker beds) all the way, and making a map of their location.

In some places, it is possible to view a cliff from a single vantage point for a half hour and map several marker beds for a mile along that cliff before finding a new vantage point to see the next mile of cliff. However, the Wyoming country is often not kind to a researcher. In other places, the terrain is rolling hills with much sagebrush cover, and rock layers have been tilted by earth movements just enough to make the task confusing. At times, this meant spending a week or two to map only about a square mile, working back and forth over the area and puzzling over the exposed rock layers. One side of the area seemed clear, but after I moved across the hills, the identity of some layers was uncertain. Then it was necessary to go back to where it was clear, study the character of those layers and their fossils, and then work back again across the area. I couldn't let the rocks get the best of me but continued until the puzzle pieces all fit together.

Spending so much time in the wilderness brought small incidental sideshows. One morning after camping along an off-road trail, I opened the back of the Suburban to fix breakfast. A hummingbird flew into the vehicle to examine a red object, mistaking it for a red flower. I still wonder how a hummingbird could survive in that desolate place in midsummer. As far as I could see, there were no flowers for miles around.

Another evening, as it was getting dark, I was surprised by a truck coming along the trail in the middle of nowhere. It turned out to be an electricity service truck following the small power line that crossed the hills. The line served a marina and camping area by Flaming Gorge Reservoir. The electricity was out at the camping area, and the technician was "trolling" the power line, searching for the cause of the problem. In the deepening darkness, he stopped about a half mile away and was joined by another truck. After an hour of work, they had the problem solved and went back to the comforts of home.

In the middle of one of those long field seasons, I went home for a weekend to give a lecture. The short drive to Salt Lake City was followed by a flight to Southern California. Then on Sunday, it was the reverse, ending back in camp at dusk. Arriving at camp, I felt an odd feeling, a sense of deep loneliness that swept over me and crept down deep inside. Yes, it was lonely out there, but I had never experienced this emotion in all the years of research in Wyoming. The intense loneliness didn't last long, and I think I know what caused it. All other research trips had begun with a fourteen- to seventeen-hour drive. That was sufficient time to make the mental and emotional transition from home and family to camping out in the sagebrush. On this occasion, I had only a two-hour flight and then the short drive from Salt Lake City to camp. It was like being jerked away from home and unceremoniously dumped into the wilderness.

The ultimate result of my mapping was clear—almost all of the dozen marker beds covered all, or almost all, of the basin. Now the relationships between the rock units in Bridger Unit B were much clearer. These sedimentary deposits were produced by processes extending over all of the nearly one thousand square miles of the basin and not by local events. That was the answer to one of our important questions about the Bridger. Another side of this project that seemed ironic was that careful mapping by a creationist would now facilitate the research of other paleontologists studying the evolution of mammals!

As I mentioned earlier, the fossil-rich Bridger Formation had been well known to scientists ever since the railroad came through in 1869. Why had no other geologists mapped the Bridger Formation in all that time? I believe an important part of the answer is that the conventional evolutionary paradigm fed the belief that these sediments and limestones formed in the same way such features are likely to form today— primarily in local ponds and lakes. If that were true, it would not be possible to map them across the basin, and parts of the Bridger with sagebrush-covered, rolling hills encouraged that view. It took someone willing to question accepted paradigms to think it might be worth trying to map the limestones.

A geologist from a nearby state university and his graduate student had realized the potential for this project and continued the mapping into Bridger C to E. They are not creationists, but careful scientists can collaborate on research, even if they have quite different views of earth history. We were all seeking accurate geological explanations, and our different viewpoints could cause each of us to see things the other might miss and thus help us avoid mistakes.

9

LAKES, TURTLES, AND VOLCANOES

After the work in the Bridger Formation, our evidence pointed to basin-wide sedimentary processes, but we still did not know how to explain some other things. Could we find the right evidence to enable us to fit it all together into a satisfying theory? That question prompted me to return to Wyoming for another summer of interrupting the peaceful rest of the fossil turtles in the Bridger Formation.

The summer research team was bigger than usual and a refreshing mix of persons. Tom Goodwin would be with us again for much of the trip. We had the able help of Albert—a new graduate student from Nebraska—and four undergraduate research assistants. They were Sam from Japan, Judy and Karen from California, and Meredith from Arkansas. Paul Buchheim was with us for two weeks, with his two sons and two students—Matthew from Tennessee and Aimee from California. It promised to be a lively summer!

Since we now knew that the green turtle layer—renamed more officially the Black Mountain turtle layer (BMtl)—continued all around the basin, it didn't take us long to devise the next phase of our research. We chose twenty research sites distributed in a big semicircle all along the BMtl, beginning at Devil's Playground and continuing along the base of Cedar Mountain, around the north end of the BMtl exposures, and finally, back along its western edge toward the Uinta Mountains. At each site, we again measured the length and width of good exposures, counted turtle bones, and calculated the number of turtle bones per hectare (this time, the number of bones, not the number of turtles). While we counted bones, Paul and his students carefully measured a section through the BMtl and up to a volcanic tuff unit (a tuff is a layer of volcanic ash, carried by the wind and then dropped) about twelve to fifteen meters above it. Our data reinforced the conclusion that the turtles were not in local concentrations but rather formed a basin-wide pattern. The number of turtle bones was about 17,000 per hectare in the southern sites, steadily decreasing to 2,000 in the northern sites. Whatever process affected the bone distribution, it was a uniform process across all the several hundred square miles of the BMtl. That was a surprising and helpful piece of evidence.

We often encountered wildlife in our travels in the Bridger. An unexpected encounter occurred when Tom began a pilot project to find small vertebrate bones called microvertebrates. He brought several five-gallon buckets of mudstone to camp and filled the buckets with water to dissolve the mudstone and release the fossils. When we came back to camp in the evening, he was surprised by how much water seemed to have evaporated during the day. He refilled the buckets, and then we enjoyed our supper and relaxed around the table.

As darkness fell, a surprise guest appeared from the other side of a hill. A moose made its way to the buckets of muddy water. When it saw us, it quickly disappeared, but we now knew how the water had "evaporated." This was far away from regular moose habitat, but moose and elk will, at times, make long journeys from one mountain range or river to another. Our moose seemed to be on such a journey and appreciated the refreshment at this stopping place—a little muddy but still refreshing. The moose needed to be moving along because it was a long way to the next moose habitat and water source.

Another day began with the sight of an elk that was also making a long journey. More common local residents are the pronghorns, sometimes incorrectly called pronghorn antelopes. They are very fast and graceful; in fact, under ideal running conditions, they are reported to approach seventy miles per hour. In the sagebrush, that speed was not likely, but sometimes when pronghorn began running parallel to us, we couldn't resist racing it. That morning we drove along the off-road trail at forty-five miles per hour as a pronghorn ran alongside through the sagebrush without tripping and then crossed over the trail ahead of us.

The railroad through Bridger country is rich in history. The first transcontinental railroad, completed in 1869, is the one that still goes across southern Wyoming, through the towns of Rock Springs and Green River and across the Bridger Formation. We often encountered the railroad in the course of our research. The railroad bed in use now is mostly the same one built in that first race between the Union Pacific and Central Pacific railway companies to increase their share of the railroad. The incentive for them was the land given to them by the government—every other square mile, for ten miles on each side of the railway. The only changes to the rail line since then have been made to allow the trains to go faster. The railroad companies have eliminated the sharper turns and replaced the original rails with heavier ones. They also replaced the original wood trestles with concrete-and-steel bridges.

Driving along beside the railroad with my imagination running free, I could almost see the old steam locomotives chugging along the tracks, with Native Americans watching warily from behind the hills—or Buffalo Bill and his riders on their graceful horses chasing herds of bison through the sagebrush to provide food for the railroad crew. Where the railroad crosses creeks, the remains of the wood trestles are often still visible under the newer concrete bridges. The railroad workers simply cut off the top of the old wood piles and left the remainder. In some places where new cuts through the hills have created more gentle turns, the old abandoned railroad bed can still be seen nearby.

Our reason for being there was turtles, and we had found that the turtles are found in specific layers just above limestones. We needed careful, quantitative documentation of that pattern. The first day after all the students arrived, we spent the day counting turtle bones up the face of Devil's Playground. With little plastic flags, we marked a path a hundred meters wide from the bottom of the hill up to the Sage Creek Limestone—the top of Unit B. Then we counted all fossils in that transect. The upper part of the hill was steep and a little slippery. I wondered whether this was a good project for the students' first day in the field, but we accomplished the task without incident. Above the turtles of the lower turtle layer, the golden bench limestone, and BMtl was only one more turtle bonanza in the Bridger Unit B—the upper turtle layer. Virtually all turtles are in these mass-death layers.

On these trips with students, a sort of personality of the group tends to emerge that is different with each mix of persons. That summer, the group was hard-working but very social. This seemed to be influenced especially by two girls who became fast friends during the trip—Judi and Meredith. Both were willing workers but also full of energy and fun. The group couldn't possibly become socially stale with them around. When Paul and his students arrived, it became even more interesting to watch, since his student assistant, Matthew, was of interest to the girls. Matthew, however, was unusually independent-minded and didn't fall for their charms.

Some months after the field season ended, I learned of an incident that occurred one Friday evening during the field trip. The professors had gone to bed, and Judi and Meredith decided to go for a walk. They went by themselves, it was reported to me, because they wanted to show they could do this without the guys helping them find their way. They climbed the small hill behind the camp and went up onto a sagebrush plateau surrounded by low hills. They were gone for a long time, and finally, Matthew became concerned. Once you climb up onto that plateau and the lights from camp are not visible, everything can look the same. He took his flashlight and went looking. Sure enough, the girls were lost up there and were glad to see the light appear. This is what one of the guys told me, and I have learned that it doesn't exactly match the adventuresome girls' version of the story.

Now we knew the turtles were killed in mass mortalities, buried quickly in mudstones right above limestones, and then there were no more turtles until another mudstone was deposited above a limestone. What could cause this repeating pattern? It indicated a repeating ecological situation associated with repeating lethal conditions for the turtles, after which no more turtles were to be found until the pattern began once more. Intriguing!

After much thought, an explanation took shape. Limestones are produced in water, and they indicated that the entire basin was periodically covered by water. It has been known for many years that the sand, clay, and silt in the sediments are from a volcanic source. These sediments have been moved around by water, and their mineral makeup has been altered, except for the tuffs, made of wind-carried ash, which then fell to the ground. Originally, most of the sediment came from the volcanic field to the north, around Yellowstone National Park.

According to our explanation, when the valley was filled with a shallow lake with many live turtles, a massive series of volcanic eruptions began. The volcanic ash or gases killed the turtles, and the volcanic sediment soon buried the turtles in the initial mudstones accumulating in the lake. The volcanic episodes continued, filling the lake and depositing more mudstone and sandstone, many yards thick. Finally, the volcanic episodes ended, another lake filled the basin, and the cycle began all over again.

According to published radiometric dates from volcanic tuff layers in the basin, an average of 200,000 years passed between the formation of one limestone layer and the next higher limestone. But if that were correct, why didn't the population of turtles build up again after each initial volcanic eruption? The sediments seemed to indicate habitats suitable for turtles, so why were turtles found only in the first few yards above each limestone? It seemed more likely that little time passed from one lake with its limestone, to the next lake and limestone. Our data doesn't demonstrate this, so we can't publish this conclusion in any scientific research paper, but the evidence and implication are very strong. This type of evidence makes the conventional geological time scale unsatisfying to some of us.

My interest in the Bridger turtles had begun with the argument between colleagues I had heard in Rock Springs. Had my question been answered? Was the Bridger Formation deposited in the biblical flood—or afterward? Scientific research often answers some of our questions and leaves other questions to be tackled later. Research may also answer questions we hadn't even thought of. That was our experience in the Bridger research. As in the sandstone trackway research, the scientific papers on the Bridger Formation contained much valuable information. However, more remained to be discovered, and our biblical worldview is what led us to make these discoveries. Our more catastrophic view of earth history led us to question the published conclusions that the limestones represented local water bodies and caused us to pursue more careful study of the actual distribution of the limestones and the turtles, seeking a reliable answer. The evidence indicated that the turtles perished in several mass-death events and were buried within a few months after each mass death. The evidence also poses some challenges to the standard geological timescale for this rock formation because it implies rapid deposition of the sediments.

If this formation was produced during the one year of the biblical flood, the origin of the entire Bridger Formation could have taken only a few weeks to form, at most. The evidence is hard to reconcile with millions of years, but it also doesn't seem compatible with forming the whole formation in a few weeks or months. Perhaps it was part of the somewhat catastrophic conditions in the hundreds of years after the Flood. Proof is not what science could give us, but this explanation is what fits the evidence in a consistent and meaningful picture.

10

DO YOU WANT TO SEE SOME FOSSIL WHALES?

Picture in your mind walking through a desolate place, entering a valley, and finding numerous complete, beautiful large fossils just waiting for you to study them. I have dreamed this type of scenario. Sometimes it was a dream, and on other occasions, I imagined this actually happening. When this dream becomes a reality, it is a wonderful opportunity to honor God by demonstrating that a creationist can do research as carefully as anyone else.

I began visiting Peru to speak at creation conferences in 1993, just as President Fujimori was bringing the war with the "Shining Path" guerillas to an end. The country had been under stress for some years, with bombings in the streets of Lima. At the campus of Universidad Peruana Unión (UPeU), a Seventh-day Adventist university on the outskirts of Lima, construction and repairs were underway across the campus, making up for the lost years when such work had not been possible. The campus is at the base of the Andes foothills, and a steep, rugged ridge above campus had been a significant route for the guerillas traveling to Lima. A tower of the power line on top of the ridge that had been bombed by the Shining Path remained fallen on the ground. Our hosts told us not to climb on that hillside "because they will shoot first and ask questions later." We didn't argue with those instructions. In Lima, most of the taxis were VW Beetles, old and patched many times, with unpainted repairs.

The beat-up Volkswagen taxis in Lima, Peru, at the end of the era
of the government's fight with the Shining Path guerillas.

In 1998, several colleagues and I again traveled to Peru to present lectures at creationism conferences in Lima and at UPeU. Peru was quieter now, and we could climb the hills behind campus to see fascinating ruins of a pre-Inca fort on top of the hill. The battered VW taxis in Lima had vanished, replaced by new Toyotas. I was there to give several talks, including a presentation on fossil trackways in the Coconino SS. We arrived on Friday, several days before the first conference, because our hosts had arranged a geology tour for a group of their students and us.

Upon our arrival at UPeU, one of the conference leaders asked a seemingly innocent question. He said that during the geology tour, we would visit a university on the high plateau in the Andes, and he asked if I would be willing to give a brief talk to some students on the limitations of science. I have written on this topic, but I hadn't prepared a talk for this occasion. It sounded like an informal, last-minute plan to talk to a few students, so I agreed. On Saturday night, with the distraction of the UPeU students having a lively party on the lawn outside of my dormitory window, I planned the talk.

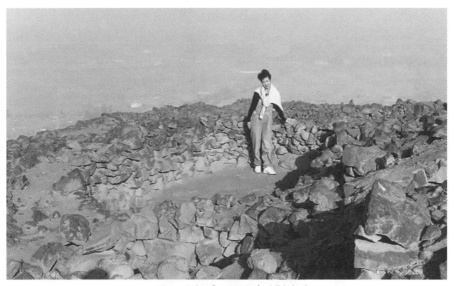

An ancient Indian fort on top of a hill behind
Universidad Peruana Unión (UPeU) in Peru.

Sunday morning, our fifty-two-passenger bus took us toward the Andes mountain range. The highway wound its way up a long river valley, climbing toward Ticlio, a pass over the ridge of the Andes at the breathtaking elevation of 16,000 feet. This is the highest highway and railroad pass in the world in regular use. On a previous trip I had taken to this same pass, someone had recommended we drink some coca tea. I didn't like the sound of it and didn't drink any. At that high elevation in the thin air, I had been so sick I could only sit in the bus in misery, hoping we would go back soon. On this second trip, I decided I would drink whatever they gave us!

As we drove past small towns in the river valley, two drunk men in a

Toyota weaved their way ahead of us. Suddenly, they wandered too far to the left and ran head on into a big truck loaded with heavy metal ingots from a mine in the Andes. Their car rebounded right in front of the bus, and our driver was barely able to stop and avoid hitting them from behind. The collision broke the truck's steering tie rod on the left front wheel. From my seat right behind the bus driver, I could see the truck driver struggling to control the truck. But it was no longer controllable, and it struck the side of our bus, bouncing along the side. When it was past the bus, the truck pursued its leftward course, swerving off the side of the road and through a heavy concrete barrier into someone's front yard. After a while, paramedics arrived and worked over the badly injured men in the Toyota and took them away.

Ticlio, the 16,000-foot-high pass over the Andes in Peru.

As I thought about the experience, I realized that had we been fifty yards farther back when the collision occurred, the truck would have hit us head on, and the driver and those of us in the front seats would have been history. Sometimes, only a split second separates life and death. A couple of years later, we saw the results of a collision of a truck and a bus, similar to the one we had been through. The truck plowed fifteen feet back through the driver's side of the bus. On our field trip, I had been sitting about five feet behind the front of the bus.

The wrecked car right in front of our bus,
on the highway above Lima, Peru.

A new bus and driver arrived, and we continued our journey. This driver told us he loved adventure, and that was obvious as he threaded his way along winding mountain roads. We took a side trip to see a cave. The narrow dirt road, cut into a steep hillside, was not made for big buses. The driver was enjoying it, however, as he moved to the far right side of the road to miss the overhanging rocks on the left and then quickly moved left to miss a man and burro walking along the road, right at the top edge of a precipice, unperturbed by the close call.

Up on the high plateau along the east side of the high mountain ridge, we made another side trip to an isolated area to examine the rocks. Two soldiers met us and accompanied us on our short hike. The state police had been informed of our visit and sent the soldiers to protect us.

Back in the bus, we made our way along the side of a large, shallow lake sprawled across the plateau. Our destination was a little stone church beside the lake, with fossils in its limestone walls. The route around the lake was not a highway but a two-track, like the off-road trails we had traveled in Wyoming. Our bus driver was again enjoying the adventure of driving as he steered over an off-road trail through the rolling countryside. Once past the church, we continued around the lake toward a bridge that crossed the river at the end of the lake. The plan was to follow this wilderness route to the town where we would spend the night in a typical Quechua house, heated by burning dried llama dung.

The truck that hit the car on the highway above Lima, Peru.

We had a long distance to drive around the lake, and I began to wonder what kind of bridge we would find on this off-road trail. As darkness was approaching, I calculated how long it would take, if the bridge were unsatisfactory, for us to go back around the lake to get to our night's lodging. It didn't look encouraging, and we were all hungry. That morning, each of us had received a plastic bag with some food in it. We finally realized that this was the only food we were going to get until evening. I don't know what kind of stomachs Peruvians have, but the rest of us needed more food. At noon, we got by with extra cheese and bread that some had wisely brought, but hunger was calling out for more.

Finally, we reached the "bridge," which was simply a flat slab of concrete with six-inch-high curbs along each side. Was that bridge designed for fifty-two-passenger buses? Was it even wise to try this? A major problem was the turn onto the bridge. The narrow "road" was cut into the side of a hill and then made a sharp right-angle turn onto the bridge, along a precipice next to the swift-flowing river. The driver began working on that turn, repeatedly driving as far forward as he dared, then backing up, trying to maneuver around to make the turn onto the bridge. I was again sitting in the front seat (you would think I might learn!), and each time he drove forward, I could look almost straight down through the darkness into the cold, raging river below. Finally, he stopped and got out to look the situation over. The bus passengers seemed to have the same thought, and we all bailed out of the bus. We watched from a safe distance as the driver continued the unlikely task. Finally, he carefully got the bus far to the left, with the front bumper hanging over the side of the bridge, so the back wheels were barely on the right side of the bridge. We were soon safely across, and dinner was not far away!

The next day, after more study of geology in these volcanic mountains, we reached the university in Cerro de Pasco, a mining city high in the Andes. After the bus was parked, we found our way into the back of one of the university buildings, where, I thought, I was to talk to a few students. I was dressed in my field clothes, looking like the stereotypical university professor on a trip, and I thought it should go well. Finally, someone led us onto the stage of a large amphitheater filled with students and professors.

To my shock, a line of people was on the stage dressed in suits, alongside me in my jeans and boots. The university president gave the first intro-duction, followed by the dean of the graduate school and several others. The event was introduced as an international symposium, and the printed bulletin didn't look as if this was a last-minute event but rather had been planned long before I heard that I was the speaker.

The presentation actually went well, in spite of my lack of awareness of what I had stepped into. I had carefully planned the end of the talk to leave the audience thinking, but I worded it so as not to unnecessarily upset secular people. I summarized the strengths and limitations of science and said that science can discover many valuable things but that I look in other places for answers to my questions about morals, values, and the origin of living things.

In the discussion time, a student picked up on that point, as I hoped someone would. He asked where I looked for answers to those questions. I replied that different people looked in various places for such answers, but I look to my religion for those answers. No negative murmuring came from the crowd, and I noticed a number of heads nodding in approval. In Peru, it seemed, less prejudice prevails against religion and creationists.

At the end, university representatives gave me a large, beautiful copper-and-wood plaque with my name engraved on it, and it, too, did not look as if it had been made at the last minute.

Wood and copper plaque given to Leonard Brand after his lecture at the university
in the city of Cerro de Pasco, high in the Andes of Peru.

After the bus took us back to Lima, we had one more free day before the conferences. A theology professor from UPeU asked us, "Do you want to see some fossil whales?" When a non-scientist asks a question like that, it can often be quite uncertain as to what they mean. On another occasion, a local person had taken us to see giant fossil clams. These were big—about two feet in diameter—but they were rock concretions, not fossils!

Since we were polite guests, we said, "Sure, we want to see the whales." A long drive followed to the city of Ica, about three hundred kilometers south of Lima, and then we traveled another forty-five minutes farther south to the little village of Ocucaje. Dusk was uncomfortably close as we arrived at the home of Chalaco, a local farmer living at the base of a line of unique whitish hills. The university theologian knew the Adventist pastor in Ica, who knew the farmer Chalaco, and Chalaco lived next door to the whales. Since it was getting late, Chalaco declined to take us up the hill with his tractor, so we walked with him. Along the base of the hill were several large objects, and they were definitely fossil whales. It hadn't been a wild goose chase after all.

A huge fossil whale in the Pisco Formation, Peru.

We eagerly followed Chalaco farther up the hill, where we saw sixteen more whales. We were able to inspect the fossils for about an hour and a half before we made our way down the hill in darkness. Many of the whales were complete and beautifully preserved—a paleontologist's bonanza!

The whales were in a white, powdery material that we learned was diatomite—the accumulation of untold billions of microscopic skeletons of aquatic diatoms. Four of us in the group were paleontologists and geologists, and we immediately decided some research was needed there and began to plan for it. Eventually, two of us in that group did follow up with the research plans, and our study in succeeding years led to more exciting discoveries than we could have expected. Those sixteen whales were only the tip of the proverbial iceberg.

Dreams sometimes do come true, but not always in the way we expect. A valley full of dinosaurs would be fascinating, but it's hard to beat a desert full of wonderful whale fossils, just waiting for us to discover their story.

Leonard Brand and his family, 1996.

$$\textcircled{11}$$

DISARTICULATING JEEPS AND BEAUTIFUL, ARTICULATED FERNANDA

After we saw the fossil whales in Peru and learned more about their presumed geological history, we were struck by an incongruity. Most of the whales are articulated skeletons and very well preserved. The published literature on them interprets the diatom-rich sediment to have been deposited only a few inches in thickness per thousand years, as happens in the oceans today. If that were true, it would have taken many thousands of years to bury a whale. However, when whales die in today's oceans, scavengers strip off the soft tissues in a few months, and the bones are soon damaged by scavengers and destroyed within a few years. Well-preserved whales and slow burial don't fit together, because rapid burial is needed to prevent scavenging and decay.

Why had this problem not been noticed by other geologists and paleontologists who had studied these Peruvian whales during the preceding twenty years? When a researcher's worldview is wrong, it can hinder him or her from asking the right questions and noticing things not expected in that worldview. In some cases, unusual things may get noticed, but their significance isn't realized. If someone is fully convinced the rocks formed slowly over millions of years, it may be very hard for that person to see evidence that doesn't fit well in that time frame.

Of the four of us who saw the whales in 1998, Art Chadwick and I pursued the whale fossil project, along with other collaborators from time to time. Art became a valued research collaborator, with his abounding energy, his habit of independent, critical thought, and his commitment to his Lord and to the Word of God. A Loma Linda University doctoral student wished to be included in the whale project for his dissertation research, and our plans began to take shape. The student, Raul Esperante, was from Spain, and his facility with Spanish was our first blessing.

To be successful in this venture, we also needed Peruvian colleagues, so it would be a joint Peruvian and US venture. We had arranged for this contingency during the previous trip. Our Peruvian collaborators were Orlando Poma, a geologist at UPeU, and a couple of other UPeU faculty. In addition to their help in the research, they would help us with their knowledge of local requirements for research permits from the government, sources of supplies and equipment, and other vital matters. An Adventist pastor in the town of Ica arranged some of our logistics, including a family home in which we could stay (which continued to be a blessing on future trips), the rental of a Jeep Cherokee, and an airplane ride so we could take aerial photos of our research area.

We arrived in Lima Thursday night and spent what remained of the night at UPeU. I thought the Jeep would be available for us on Friday or that we could pick it up at a rental agency. However, a bus belonging to the Adventist Development and Relief Agency (ADRA) took us the three hundred kilometers south to Ica, and when we arrived at our home, the Jeep was already there, having been rented from a friend of the pastor. At first glance, it looked good, but on closer inspection, we found that the key was broken partway across the middle; the right-side mirror hung down, held on by a cable; and the tires were almost bald and had some loose flaps of rubber with broken steel belts visible underneath. There was no spare tire. The Jeep tailgate had to be propped open with a broom handle, and the seat belts didn't work. We also found that the steering wheel had a lot of play in it, which can be pretty tricky in town, where the traffic follows the law of the jungle. The tires were especially of concern since on research trips into the wilderness, tires and a spare tire are always a critical lifeline.

Saturday (Sabbath) afternoon, while we were on a drive in our Jeep, the frightening thought occurred to me that the pastor who had arranged the Jeep rental was the same person who had arranged for one of his friends to give us an airplane ride the next day. I asked the pastor if the airplane was in better shape than the vehicle. His answer was not encouraging. He said, "More or less. Here in Peru, all cars, buses, and planes run on faith." The good news was that the plane turned out to be in excellent condition, and the pilot was very competent, an employee of a tourist agency that takes people to see the Nazca lines.

The Jeep that survived research trips only
through prayer, at the Pisco Formation, Peru.

But we still had our car problem to deal with. Saturday night, the pastor and a friend of his took it to a mechanic to have it checked out, and the mechanic said it was fine (by his standards).

On Sunday and Monday, we had no choice but to drive to the field and pray for our tires. Monday, two crew members left us at our research site and drove back to Ica to look for tires. No tires of the right size could be found in Ica, so they called a relative in Lima and arranged for the purchase of tires and a wheel so we could have a spare. Those wouldn't arrive until Tuesday evening, so we still had to drive on faith for another day—and that wasn't all. After looking for tires, they had the Jeep checked out some more. The engine had very little oil, so that was remedied. The water in the radiator was rusty, so they had it changed and added some antifreeze. The transmission had no oil! They added oil. Why hadn't it frozen up already? We promised ourselves we would just drive and ask no more questions about the car.

We wondered why the Jeep had such trouble making it up the high, sandy hill we climbed each day. Then we discovered it was because the four-wheel drive didn't work. In addition, the clutch slipped, and the smell it gave off was not promising.

On Wednesday, we took the new tires to a shop to have them installed. Before we got to the shop, we two Americans were dropped off out on the street, because if we were at the tire shop, the price for the work would be higher. Later we heard from a colleague that a mechanic squeezed one tire with his hand, and air came out from one of the broken places in the rubber. He said, "I don't know how you could have driven on these tires!" But we know it was the One above who kept the tires together.

Now we had decent tires, but we still had that slipping clutch and no time to spare to leave the Jeep in the shop. During the entire trip, the clutch was slipping and smelled as if it were overheating. Each day, the Jeep struggled up the hill, and we proceeded with our work.

During this daily drama with the Jeep, we spent our days looking for whales. We didn't have to look far, and it quickly became evident that we had only just begun to realize the abundance of whales in the Pisco Formation, as the area is called. It was a wonderful place for the study of geology and fossils because it never rains in the region. I'm not saying it seldom rains—it doesn't rain ever! This is part of the Atacama Desert, the driest desert in the world. No rain and no plants to cover the rocks and fossils—a paleontologist's paradise. The area is a coastal plain, about 1,500 feet above sea level, along the base of the Andes. People can live only along the rivers coming from the Andes to the Pacific Ocean. Our host family lived in the large town of Ica on the Ica River.

On this trip, we had a little less than two weeks for our work, so we hoped to accomplish a lot in a short time. We chose a steep hillside to begin acquainting ourselves with the Pisco Formation sediments. Because of surface erosion, we had to clean off the surface to expose the fresh hillside underneath. We measured a section and collected rock samples. After working our way up the lower part of the hillside, we looked farther up to plan our next steps. As we looked over the bare hillside, something didn't look right. It seemed that the series of distinctive layers near us also appeared higher up the hill. A little more scouting revealed that we had begun our study on a large slump block—a slab of the steep hillside that had broken loose and slid down the hill. The layers near us were indeed repeated higher up the hill.

We didn't have time to spend on wandering pieces of hillside, so we went up the hill above Chalaco's farm to the place we had first visited the year before. We explored the broad hilltop, called Cerro Blanco (white hill), placing numbered plastic flags by each fossil whale and taking a GPS reading on its position. Raul and I walked through a flat area along one side of the hill. We came to call it Whale Valley because of the number of whales there. We walked along a draw at the edge of Whale Valley, and I said to Raul, "We need to find a whale for excavating—a whale that is almost all covered and is only beginning to be exposed at the surface." About two minutes later, he excitedly called me to see one he had found on the flats above the little draw. It was perfect! The ground surface was quite level, and only the top of the front part of the whale's snout and the top of a few vertebrae were visible. The rest was buried, but not very deep.

Our crew in 2001 consisted of Raul, Art, two faculty members from UPeU—Orlando and Merling—and me. The digging in the diatomaceous sediment was not difficult, and in a couple of days the whale, which we called Fernanda, was exposed so we could examine it closely. Fernanda was a beauty. It was all there except for a couple of vertebrae at the end of the tail. The finger bones, or phalanges, from one flipper were missing, probably because they had been at ground level and were eroded away or taken by someone. The rest of the bones were in their normal articulated positions and were very well preserved. Several shark teeth were in close proximity to the whale bones, and the point of one shark tooth was embedded in the whale skull. The scavengers had not torn the whale bones loose from the skeleton, but they must have removed a lot of flesh in a hurry.

Periodically, some of our crew took a break from digging up bones and searched for more whales, marking them and taking their GPS position. By the next-to-last day before we finished, we had located ninety-eight whales. I wondered why Raul wanted to spend precious time on the last day looking for more whales. Of course, he had to find whales number 99 and 100!

The sediment enclosing a fossil also contains important clues to the fossil's history. We examined the sediment around the whale, collected samples for lab analysis, and dug a small trench in the sediment across the middle of the whale so we could see features inside the sediment. The evidence indicated the whale carcass had settled on the bottom of the bay as a water current flowed from the front to the back of the whale. The current scoured out a shallow depression, and the whale settled into the depression and was quickly covered. Just how quickly was indicated by the well-preserved bones, which would have been badly damaged by invertebrate scavengers in a few months if the whale hadn't been quickly covered. Fernanda, like the other whales in the Pisco, didn't even have any fossils of invertebrate scavengers near it. A slab of baleen was carried from the whale's mouth, by the current, and settled on top of a flipper. This baleen still contained unfossilized protein, a further indication of how quickly it was buried. Baleen is not bone but keratin, which is rapidly destroyed when whales die today.

All of this evidence confirmed our initial suspicions that the whales were buried too quickly to be damaged much by scavenging or by extensive decay. That evidence is important, but to get our work published, we needed to have a realistic theory to explain the evidence. So now we had to figure out how so many whales could be concentrated in this area and how the diatoms could accumulate that fast. Lots of reading and thinking would be necessary back home.

The research crew excavating the whale we named
Fernanda, at the Pisco Formation, Peru.

On the last day of the trip, the Jeep's clutch was worse than ever and smelled bad. We roared up the hill to keep going through the sand with our two-wheel drive, turning the loose steering wheel rapidly back and forth to keep on the track and praying for that clutch. We made it almost all the way up the hill and parked it facing downhill, just in case. We walked the remaining distance, finished the research we needed to accomplish for the trip, and came back to the Jeep, feeling elated with our success. Then Raul tried to start the jeep, but there was no response—it was dead. The lights had not been left on, but the battery had no life. We tried to start it by rolling the vehicle downhill, but no luck. Raul asked me to try, so I did. It would not start, and engaging the clutch didn't seem to make any difference at all. Apparently, the battery and clutch were nonfunctional.

Fortunately, the track was more or less downhill, so in the gathering darkness, we got the Jeep to begin rolling. Somehow it kept rolling, even though the track wasn't all downhill. We rolled down to Chalaco's home

at the base of the hill. Chalaco's son Willey offered to take us to town, but
his army-style Jeep had a broken battery cable. We gave him one from
our Jeep, and we jammed ourselves into his little open Jeep with seats for
four, though there were five of us plus our research gear and Willey. We
bounced over the farm trails in the moonlight to the village of Ocucaje.
There, we found an old bus heading for Ica. So ended our adventure with
the Jeep Cherokee—almost.

Leonard Brand and Fernanda.

That evening, I asked one of our Peruvian colleagues a question I had
been afraid to ask before: Did the Jeep have any insurance? He said no,
that was unlikely. We also learned the pastor had signed an agreement to
be fully responsible for the Jeep. If we'd had an accident, what then? Of
course, we would have carried the full responsibility. The pastor may not
have understood such matters, but he did have a lot of faith, and his faith
was rewarded.

The next day, the Jeep was towed to Ica, and a mechanic found that
the battery had not been fastened down and was bouncing against the fan
blade. It ceased working because the fluid drained through the hole in the
side of the battery. The clutch was burned out and needed to be replaced.
We also learned that the drive shaft for the four-wheel drive wasn't even
in the car anymore! Certainly, Someone was watching over that Jeep and
us to keep us going (for $50 per day) until we didn't need the vehicle
anymore—and then it just died.

12

SERGIO

In the years after 1999, we made two additional trips to Peru for Raul to finish his data collection on the whales and for another student to finish a master's thesis on the sedimentology of the Pisco Formation. We now had data on more than 420 whales. We also met Sergio, a Peruvian vertebrate paleontologist who became our research collaborator and treasured friend. We learned to trust our safety to his knowledge of Peru and its people.

Our evidence indicated that the whales apparently died from suffocation by volcanic ash during the formation of the Andes Mountains or from toxins produced by massive blooms (red tides) of diatoms and other organisms in the ocean. The whales then drifted into shallow bays, sank to the bottom, and were buried rapidly by accumulating diatom-rich sediment. Later, the entire area was raised up, along with the Andes Mountains, to form a coastal plain available for us to study.

The evidence was clear: the whales were not buried slowly over many thousands of years but were each buried within weeks or months after their death. That required diatom accumulation several orders of magnitude faster (a million times faster) than previously believed. How would I convince the scientific community? Would that idea ever get published?

I spent most of a summer studying the scientific literature on diatoms and was gratified as a theory began to take shape, supported by published evidence about diatoms. Certain factors could reasonably account for such rapid diatom accumulation, from tremendous plankton blooms attracting many whales to this food source to storms (as evidenced in the sediment) concentrating both whales and diatoms in the shallow bays, where they sank to the bottom.

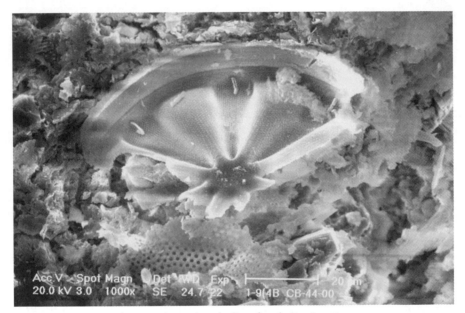

A scanning electron photo of a diatom from the Pisco Formation.
The material around it is mostly broken diatoms.

We shared our evidence and theory with some of the best vertebrate taphonomy experts and diatom experts, and they agreed that the data supported our theory. They also helped us to strengthen the weaker parts of the theory. All of this evidence was then published in the prestigious journal *Geology*, with a photo of our whale Fernanda on the cover. It wasn't appropriate in such a publication to indicate that our belief in the Bible inspired our research, but that was objectively true. The data were gathered in proper scientific fashion, and they supported our conclusions, which is good science. And although many scientists firmly believe that a creationist could never truly be a scientist, the biblical source of our ideas was a help rather than a hindrance to good science, done with standard approaches to collecting and analyzing data.

The Pisco Formation in our study area is several hundred meters thick, and our research up to that time had been in the upper part of the formation. In Raul Esperante's dissertation research, we had been able to show that this upper part is full of well-preserved whales that must have been rapidly buried.

Based on our experience thus far, I prepared a three-page outline of my research plan for the next phase of the work. I discussed it with Raul, and he was interested in helping with it, while also beginning some projects of his own. We wondered, What is the rest of the formation like below our early study site? Does it also have well-preserved whales? With the collaboration of Art Chadwick, Raul, and some assistants, and with the research plan ready, I was determined to seek an answer to that question.

Before we could answer the question about the whales, we had to develop a reliable way to identify where each location fits in the sequence from bottom to top of the formation. This is called the stratigraphic sequence— like reading a book and knowing which page we are on in each part of the book. In the Grand Canyon of Arizona, the whole sequence of rock layers is visible in the canyon walls. It is easy to tell which layers are at the bottom and what the sequence of all the layers is as we climb up the trails along the canyon walls. It isn't as easy to make that kind of study in a place like the Pisco, where the rocks are spread for miles across varied terrain. We would have to search the desert valleys and hills diligently, with plenty of water in our canteens, to assign "page numbers" to each part of this ancient rocky "history book." The mapping I had done in the Bridger Formation in Wyoming was good training for this task.

A plaque I once read in a gift shop said, "Man plans—God laughs." On Thursday of the week we were to leave for Peru, I arrived at the Los Angeles International Airport with three suitcases, prepared to pay extra for one, just as the agent I telephoned earlier had said I could. I learned that this could not be done on a flight to Peru. The man behind the counter could not be persuaded, so I had to reschedule my flight for the next morning and find a way to ship the suitcase—which cost $210 plus a hotel for the night. The hotel faced the runway, so I could watch the planes take off—without me!

After I arrived in Peru the next day and met Sergio and the other members of the research party, we went to stay at UPeU until early Sunday morning. An American paleontologist and veteran Pisco Formation researcher, whom I'll call Glenn, joined us for the first week. That year, we hired Gilberto, an expert Peruvian truck driver with his four-wheel-drive pickup, and he arranged for a second truck and driver as well. We figured there should be advantages in having local drivers who knew the desert well and knew where to get truck repairs.

The truck drivers arrived two and a half hours late, but we were in Peru, so we decided to just live with it. The four-hour drive took us to our host family home in Ica, where we stayed and prepared for the next few days. Then we headed south again on the Pan-American Highway. About a half hour's drive out of Ica, Glenn and I were discussing previous car problems we'd had in Peru, and he said, "Well, we are off to a good start on this trip." A few seconds later—*BAM!*—the back wheel hub dropped onto the pavement when a wheel and tire came off and rolled down the road without us. Two hours later, we were finally back on the road again.

It seemed that while the truck was parked in Lima the night before, someone had tried to steal the wheel and took off all the lug nuts that hold the wheel on. That meant we had driven through the busy streets and freeways of Lima and three hundred kilometers down the Pan-American Highway with no nuts holding the wheel on. It finally came off on a curve with no other vehicles around that could have resulted in an accident.

In Lomas, we stayed in a little private, three-room, one-bathroom hotel owned by the sister of one of our drivers. The bathroom had modern appliances, but the little fishing village of Lomas had no running water, so the only way to get water into a given appliance was to pour it from a bucket to a pitcher and then into the appliance. Our hotel owner cooked good vegetarian meals for us, and the room was only five dollars per person per night. It was better than a little hotel we had stayed in the previous year, where restrooms opening into a hallway were so small that one could use the facilities or close the door but not both at the same time.

We spent the week learning all that Glenn knew about the area and especially about fossil invertebrates, in preparation for our own work. Conditions were windy and dusty, and I noticed that after a couple of days, my hair was a nice brown color and looked quite good—I could style it any way I wished and it would stay that way. A few days later, after a shower in town, I noticed the hair treatment was not permanent.

Our camp at Cerro Brujito, which we called the Brujito Hilton because it was our most scenic camp in the Pisco Formation.

The fastest way to the next location was to drive down a little off-road trail to the beach, proceed along the beach for several miles—half in the shallow water and half out of the water—to another trail, and then back up a river valley. Along the beach were abundant animals of two types—gulls and big red crabs, several inches across. The gulls flew out over the water as we approached, but the thousands of crabs feeding in the shallow water scurried away to the sand dunes as we approached. It was a humorous sight to see as they ran away from us in groups of dozens to a hundred or more.

Having Glenn with us for the week was truly beneficial. Some of these areas were new to us, but he knew them well. We camped for a night on the way to Cerro Queso Grande—"Big Cheese Hill." When we camped, I began preparing the supper of spaghetti and mashed potatoes, when Sergio realized he needed to come to my rescue and the supper's rescue. He would be our cook for the rest of the trip when we camped.

The following week was memorable in ways good and bad. We spent a few days walking for miles, following rock layers to be sure we knew which whales on this hill were in the same layers as whales on the other hillside. One night, we experienced a rare event—the Peruvian desert equivalent of a rainstorm. Possibly, it was the worst storm in many years. At dusk, a beautiful double rainbow arched across the sky, and while Sergio was cooking spaghetti in the back of the truck, it rained as hard as it ever rains there—not enough water to chase anyone in out of the rain, but I felt a few dozen drops!

Breakfast at the Brujito Hilton. Around the truck are Orlando Poma,
Leonard Brand, and our valued collaborator, Sergio.

Sunday night, I took the bus to Lima, and on Monday morning went to customs to get my suitcase that had been shipped from Los Angeles by a cargo company. The previous week, we had sent Orlando Poma to retrieve the case for me, since I had put his name and mine on the shipping bill, but he found he needed my passport—or that I needed to get the suitcase myself—and he also learned we would need a lawyer. So I came back to Lima with Sergio, as my local expert on Peruvian life, and also with a lawyer sent by friends to help us. We went to customs at 8:00 A.M., and five hours and several hundred dollars later, I finally left with the suitcase.

In the suitcase was a satellite phone, and we were informed by the customs agents they are illegal in Peru. It would have taken just about as much time and money to clear the suitcase without the presence of the phone, but the phone slowed things down even more. I only received receipts for part of the customs fees, so I suspect part of the cost was for something that we don't call a fee. I was finally reunited with my boots, coat, hat, toiletries case, phone, and cans of vegetarian hot dogs. I had learned an expensive lesson in Peruvian customs practices. It would have been much cheaper if the airline agent had mentioned on the phone that some countries won't accept bringing extra suitcases on the plane.

That week at the church in Ica, the pastor asked me to give a ten-minute talk while he changed clothes after a baptism, and then he would preach the sermon. After my little talk, however, while we were standing at the podium, he told the congregation, in Spanish, that he was going to ask me to preach the sermon also. Fortunately, I had a sermon tucked in my Bible that I hadn't preached at that church before. I had two sermons, and eventually I preached them both at that church. Later I was thinking, *What will I do if he does the same thing again?* The next week at church, the pastor spared me—he had another guest preacher.

In the afternoon, the youth had a choir practice, followed by a question-and-answer time for me on the subject of Creation. The young people were full of life—it was wonderful to hear them sing. I didn't know the words for some of their songs, but I could sense the lively spirit of their love for Jesus in the singing.

Saturday night we went into town, and it was Easter weekend. The street market and the town square were full of people shopping and talking. The town pulsed with life, unlike our empty streets at home that are sometimes too quiet. The Latin beat of the music in some street shops added to the liveliness of the scene.

The past week had been a rocky start, with the suitcase problem and some difficult geological puzzles to solve. But after successfully liberating the suitcase, we now figured out the stratigraphy, or the relationship between rock layers, over a huge area. My feet were sore and blistered from walking so many miles over the desert, but at the end of it, I was in good spirits!

Orlando Poma, Leonard Brand, and Art Chadwick
with the Bendezu family, our hosts in Ica, Peru.

In the newspaper, we learned of a postscript to the suitcase situation. A day or two after we got the suitcase, a group of customs agents in Lima were arrested and put in jail for running an illegal operation on the side—sending shipping containers to places that were not their planned destinations. The article included photos of the agents, and Sergio recognized some of them as the ones with whom we had dealt in getting the suitcase—we had new friends in unexpected places!

The hosts with whom we lived in Ica, the Bendezu family, were delightful people. The couple had two junior high–aged children—a son and a daughter. They also had a cute little one-year-old boy, Obed. They taught Obed to say hi, so that he enthusiastically greeted the Americans with "Hi-i-i-i, hi-i-i!" We tried to teach him to say "Howdy," so that when Art Chadwick arrived from Texas, Obed could give him a proper Texas greeting.

The amount we paid for room, board, and laundry seemed so little compared with the cost of living in the United States, but the two older Bendezu children were able to go to church school for several years because of the money the family made hosting us on these trips. The oldest child, Nelsie, wanted to be an obstetrician, and her brother, Alex, planned to be a doctor. Our financial investment in them was money well spent.

That particular week, we camped for two nights. Sergio cooked spaghetti, "smashed" potatoes (as he called them), and dried eggs.

The next week promised to be a good one, but I would be in the field for a day or two without a Spanish translator.

13

SERGIO AND THE SPANIARD'S WIFE

Research trips outside of our native land can teach us much about the local people as well as reveal scientific discoveries. Our Peruvian paleontologist friend, Sergio, had become like part of our family. He didn't have any religious inclinations or experience as far as I could see, but he listened politely when we had morning worship, and he cooked vegetarian meals for us on camping trips.

We learned from him that he was in the middle of an international drama, with a plot that would make a great novel. Call it "Sergio and the Spaniard's Wife." Sergio had been working for many years for the Lima Natural History Museum. He had a lab there, where he prepared his fossils. The museum didn't pay him any salary—no money was available for that—but he loved what he did and found a way to make a little money here and there.

A paleontologist from Spain, whom we will call Garcia (not his real name), had been spending time at a university in Lima for about twenty years, studying the fossils in the Pisco Formation, the same formation we were studying. He had trained Sergio through the years until Sergio became the best vertebrate paleontologist in Peru. Sergio was like a desert fox—given to taking off in his moccasins with a small plastic bottle of water, wandering for hours in the desert, and finding fossils. Garcia did not treat him well, however. Sergio had to spend his own money for materials to find and prepare his fossils, and Garcia expected Sergio to provide fossils for him to describe in scientific journals so that Garcia could become more famous. Garcia did not pay Sergio anything or cover his costs for fossil preparation, although he paid his European students to come to Peru to study Sergio's fossils. He gave his European students priority over Peruvian students in the choice of who got to publish on a fossil discovery.

We paid Sergio for his excellent work with us, and he appreciated us. He became less willing to give his fossils to Garcia, and Garcia made such statements to him as, "Your country is just a colony, so you should act accordingly and hand over your fossils."

When Sergio was working for us, he found a fossil pygmy sperm whale—a new species and the only fossil of that species in the world up to that time. Garcia was beside himself, wanting to get his hands on that fossil. Instead of improving how he treated Sergio, Garcia appointed his wife as curator of fossils at the university. His wife didn't actually work there—it was just a ploy to get control of Sergio's fossils at the university.

Sergio was not going to fall for such a move, and before Garcia's wife's appointment began, he left the university and took his fossils with him. His friends helped him hide the fossils in their homes and in a Jewish synagogue. Sergio's students finished the job by going to the administration and complaining about how Garcia had treated them. They were good students from a couple of different universities in Peru, so their influence could not be ignored. The students threatened to tell the story to the press, and subsequently, Garcia was asked not to come back to Peru. The score: Sergio 1, Garcia 0.

Fortunately, we were not implicated in this soap opera in a way that put us at odds with other scientists, but I felt sorry for Sergio. He had been trying to get a group of American paleontologists who specialize in systematics and evolution interested in working with him and studying his fossils. He made some money working for us, but our field of research, taphonomy, was not the long-term solution he needed for support. He was getting a little discouraged about the prospects for a reliable income.

When we reached the halfway point in this trip to Peru, we had accomplished some good things. Two major parts of our research area were separated by a long field of huge, modern sand dunes, and we finally figured out approximately which rock layers on one side matched with those on the other side of the dune field—a lot of walking and contemplating had revealed the secret.

Leonard Brand and our favorite fossil whale,
with an entire mouthful of baleen.

The research was fascinating and rewarding, but at the same time, I looked forward to being home again. On one day, we finished counting whales and other fossils on a transect from the bottom to the top of the Pisco Formation in the area of Ocucaje, and we excavated specimens as well. Sergio worked on a complete dolphin, and the rest of us began excavating a small whale. Both were complete animals with articulated skeletons. The whale had its baleen in its mouth, and both specimens were surrounded with a rind—like a watermelon rind—of hard orange sediment (in contrast to the typical white sediment color), which was the result of chemical reactions from decaying flesh after burial. All these pointed to the rapid burial of the animals, which didn't fit easily with the long time periods most geologists want to put on these deposits. We would come back the next day to finish our whale.

I was amazed at the life-forms that existed in the desert, even though in most places, not a green bush or even grass blade was anywhere in sight. Fox tracks were common, and we saw occasional insects and lizards and one gecko and noticed occasional rodent tracks or burrows. *What did they eat?* I wondered. Missing were birds—no birds at all, once we got away from the river valleys, except for a few vultures. In town and in the river valley, I identified some birds: vultures, vermillion flycatchers (beautiful—all red and black), croaking ground doves, burrowing owls, a hummingbird, and what looked like a white-winged dove.

In the little village of Ocucaje, near our primary research site, was the very nice Ocucaje Hotel. While I think most travelers would be pleased with it, one should not think Hilton—think small Peruvian countryside resort in a little village of mud-brick houses. Sergio knew the owner, and the owner had been looking at my website and wanted to meet us. He wanted to know how he could learn more about the whales and attract more tourists to see the rich fossil resources nearby. So we stopped in and visited the hotel's owner.

It was a pleasant visit, and we thought that maybe we could help each other. It would be worthwhile for me to pay to have a whale or two collected and prepared, so we could see the fully cleaned skeletons, and the whales could attract people to his resort. I tried to find a way to have Sergio paid by the town to do the collecting and preparing, but there wasn't a reliable way to get the money to him without most of it being siphoned off into some politician's pocket. Doing it through a private party, such as the hotel owner, would be a safer approach.

At about that time, Art Chadwick arrived from Texas, and Raul Esperante from Loma Linda, along with Ronny, a graduate geology student from Italy. With three new research team members, it was time for us to take a long drive through a lot of territory we hadn't yet explored to see what new wonders we might find. Then we would begin a more detailed study of whale specimens.

Ronny was a new member of our team—a promising scholar and a Christian gentleman. He and I had some long talks about the relationship between faith and science, and I was delighted with his positive approach to these things. He would be an important asset to the work of God. He spoke good English, although I noticed that when he talked on the phone to his girlfriend, who was back in Italy, he spoke in tongues!

We found more superb whale specimens. A large one had a beautiful full mouthful of preserved baleen, well exposed as if arranged for some great photos. As I said before, fossil baleen indicates that the whale was buried quickly.

We also found a beautifully preserved fossil turtle. Its skull, front foot, and the front part of its shell were sticking out of the rock. The head, with its big eyes, was looking at us, and I thought I could hear it saying, "Help, I'm stuck in this rock!"

One day, we stopped by the open-air market in Ica on the way to work, and I accompanied Sergio as he bought groceries for our camping trip. These markets are composed of many small family shops. The family-oriented nature of the people and the atmosphere of the little markets is something I prefer over our contemporary American caveman society. We push a button in the morning, and our cave door opens. We back the car out and close the cave door. Then, in the evening, we open the cave, drive in, and close the cave door safely behind us and seldom see our neighbors. Our technology-oriented culture isolates people from each other. If we could take the open friendliness of the Peruvian culture and get rid of the corruption that is such a curse there, how nice it would be. I should acknowledge, however, that the country I am thinking of has already been described in Revelation 21 and 22. I am looking forward so much to that better land—with all the wonders of life and relationships without the effects of sin—that we can enjoy together.

14

MOTHER'S DAY ROBBERS
AND THE FIVE-STAR HOTEL

S hould I run for president of Peru? While I was on this particular trip in 2004, my friend Ed suggested in an email that I do so. I thought that being president would be a big hassle, but perhaps I could do something to reduce the political corruption there. It would also offer the unprecedented opportunity to shuffle large sums of government money into the fossil research budget!

Mother's Day on this trip turned out not to be a good day. Saturday night, the two teenage children of our host family were at the Adventist church. Their parents told us not to be surprised if we heard a racket during the night, as they suspected the pastor and the young people were planning to go around visiting church families and giving little Mother's Day celebrations at each one (a local custom). That is what they did, but they never got to our home. At one home, the pastor came out of the house and found his car tire flat. While he was changing it, he was attacked by thieves. Just then, the kids all came out of the house with their backpacks containing their church clothes. The thieves took all the backpacks and left.

Sunday morning, we left for our research site with lunches packed in a

Peruvian-style metal ice chest that sat in the back of our truck. At lunch-time, we got ready to eat and then looked for the lunch container. It was nowhere to be found, and a few irritated people started asking, "Who forgot to put the lunch container in the truck?" I stopped that by saying, "We won't ask that question. The lunches are just not here, and it will be a long afternoon, but we will make it."

When we arrived at our host's home that evening, it became clear that no one had forgotten the lunches. Somehow, on our way through town in the morning, some hungry citizen had decided he or she needed the food more than we did and stole the lunch container. That is why we don't camp in Peru unless we are way out in the wilderness, where no one knows we are there—otherwise, it isn't safe.

Another danger in Peru is earthquakes. The Adventist church in Ica was going to be torn down and rebuilt by volunteer builders. The current church, like many other buildings, was not built with reinforced concrete, and in an earthquake it would just fall down. Throughout history, earth-quakes have been common in Peru. Records tell of at least one big city and its culture ending because of a large quake several hundred years ago. In the desert, when the water supply is disrupted, that is the end.

We drove to Lima for a few days at UPeU to give a creationism symposium. The talks were well received. We also visited a government facility. Before we arrived in the country, the Peruvian equivalent of the national atomic energy commission had somehow heard we were coming and asked to visit with our whale research group. On Thursday of that week, we spent the morning with a group. I was puzzled about why the people at the atomic energy commission were interested in whale research, but it turned out their reactor and the associated facilities we visited were used entirely for research. The group at the commission wanted to know about any research going on in Peru and were looking for opportunities to collaborate with other researchers. They were using the reactor for analysis in chemistry, physics, molec-ular biology, and other areas. They especially wanted to find research that would benefit the health fields and industry. For example, they were involved in identifying disease organisms and treatment, as well as solving a problem with Peru's alpaca herds that had partly interbred with llamas, reducing the quality of their wool. They had molecular techniques for identifying the purebred alpacas.

The first thing I noticed as we came into the nuclear facility was a poster on the bulletin board announcing our creation symposium. Before the main meeting time, we were taken to a conference room and welcomed by the director of research at the facility. He said he had attended one of our creation symposia a few years earlier, and he remembered a talk by a Doctor Brand on fossil trackways that he found interesting. That was a big surprise to me. He also said that when he was a high school student, he had attended the academy at UPeU for three years.

A few days later, at the Seventh-day Adventist church in the town of Ica, a student asked me what I liked about Peru. I said it was the family-oriented culture and the way people gathered in town and in their neighborhoods to visit. Many of the people had almost nothing, but they had each other, and they talked to each other! It was quite different from our mechanized, materialistic culture that isolates so many people. A few days earlier, one of our students had been feeling sorry for the poor Peruvian people and asked Sergio what we could do to help them—what we could give them. Sergio's answer was interesting. He said, "Don't give them anything. Just leave them alone—they are happy."

We had seen a family working in a small excavation, digging out minerals, which they put in burlap bags to sell and make a little money. Sergio said, "Watch them—they have almost nothing, but they are talking and laughing together. They are happy. We should not think the people out here living in shacks are poor—they are rich—rich in culture." He said the real problem we brought was TV, with its distortion of reality. The people begin thinking they want all the stuff they see on TV, so they leave the country and go to Lima to find it. That is when they become poor in the ways that really matter. They have then lost their culture and probably won't get all the things they want.

A Peruvian farmer on his donkey with a typical set of "saddlebags."

We discovered that those of us who don't live in Peru sometimes don't know when we are collaborating unwittingly with the devil. In Peru, the selling and exporting of fossils is illegal, but professional fossil dealers were buying fossils from fossil thieves and selling them to collectors in other countries for large amounts of money. We learned that our chief truck driver, Gilberto, also drove sometimes for professional collectors, and we had been taking him to places with lots of good fossils! Even the director of the Lima Natural History Museum knew about that truck driver and was concerned about him driving for us. But it seemed too late in our trip to change drivers, so we kept working with Gilberto.

Sergio spent a couple of days collecting the best fossils he could find and then hauled them to the Bendezu home in Ica so no one could steal them. Life was never dull there! While Sergio was excavating a beautiful fossil dolphin, the truck driver came to him and suggested in a sort of double talk that they sell the fossil together. He was fascinated with that dolphin, no doubt because it could bring as much as $10,000 on the fossil black market.

Our truck driver may have had questionable ethics, but he was good at what he did. If one of the trucks got stuck in the sand, he had it out in minutes. He also drove like Jehu—furiously! The Pan-American Highway—the only north-south highway along the west side of the Andes Mountains—wound its way through several villages on the way to our research area. Shops and houses were fairly close to the highway, and people walked and cycled along the road at all times. The speed limit signs said 35 kilometers per hour, but our truck driver often went through these villages at 100 to 120 kilometers per hour! I watched his speedometer in wonder as houses and people went zipping past the truck window.

I eventually decided that if we came back to Peru for another trip, I would prefer to drive myself instead of hiring a driver, for several reasons. For one thing, I like driving there. With their traffic "suggestions" instead of traffic laws, every drive was an adventure! You had to get used to the system, and then it wasn't so bad. One had to be alert always for someone doing something crazy at any time. If a big truck was coming toward you, passing some cars on a curve across the double yellow line, you just kept smiling and moved over onto the shoulder to let the crazy truck driver go past.

We came to understand what Sergio had warned us about. He had been telling us that when we planned our travel in Peru, we should plan an extra day to get where we were going because you never knew what would happen. One Monday morning, after spending the previous evening signing autographs at the end of a symposium, we left Lima in our two trucks. The day involved driving three hundred kilometers to Ica, then another two hundred kilometers south to Lomas, the little fishing village we had visited at the beginning of the trip. The problem was that high school teachers were on strike. They were protesting that for ten years they had been paid 600 soles per month (about $175) when government officials get 10,000 soles per month, and the teachers were having some trouble understanding the reason for that differential. At the town of Chincha Alta, the strikers had closed down the Pan-American Highway. Since it is a fairly big town, we were able to find our way through back streets and get around the strikers.

But then we reached a little town where the strikers had closed the

Pan-American Highway, and the only way across the river in that town was the highway bridge. We joined a long line of trucks, buses, and cars stranded because of the strike, and no one knew how many more hours the highway would be closed. Then we thought that with our four-wheel-drive trucks, we had other options. We left the highway and took to the little dirt roads through the asparagus and cotton fields and drove until we found, with the help of local farmers, a place to drive across the river valley, through a shallow part of the river and back to the highway on the other side. The highway going south was empty—the other vehicles were all stuck back in that little town.

Rumors surfaced that a bigger strike for higher pay was in the works, involving all the truck and bus drivers and—I am not making this up—the people who worked in the cocaine fields. I hoped the transportation workers would finish striking by the time we headed for home.

We spent a week in the area around Lomas, documenting all the fossils in a 100-meter-wide band through the successive rock layers across a large valley. We hired two local workers to dig up a couple of whales for us. The whales were fascinating—they were both complete and articulated but had both been scrunched up into an "S" shape before burial. It looked as though the water current had squeezed them into that shape.

The week was one of hard work but a rewarding one. We stayed in the same little three-room hotel. To find a "five-star" hotel in that little village for five dollars per night per person was surprising. By five stars, I mean that you could look out the window at night and see five stars.

I thought this might be my last research trip to Peru unless a short trip was needed later to finish up. A couple of lifetimes of research could still be done here, but I had accomplished what I thought were the basic goals of the project. When we had started several years earlier, our attitude was, "Oh, wow, look—a whale!" But now, several hundred whales later, we were getting down to, "Oh, just another whale." When I talked of this being my last trip to Peru, Sergio laughed and told me of other paleontologists who had been saying for twenty years that they were finished and not coming back, only to continue their research trips to Peru.

15

WHO CARES ABOUT FOSSIL WHALES?

Ten more days and I would be home! This had been a great trip, but there comes a time when I start counting the days, and I had been counting for a while now. I was looking forward to seeing my family and friends again. I thought it would take some time for me to get my pictures printed, but then it dawned on me (duh!) that all the pictures were on my laptop, so I would create a slide presentation of the trip for family gatherings. I would be merciful, though, and not show all 500 pictures—I would leave perhaps a couple of them out.

On the last day in Peru for our Italian graduate student, Ronny, we finished our excavations of three whales and one bed of zillions of fossil clams and then drove to see an especially fascinating whale we had discovered earlier on this trip—the one with the great big smile and a mouth full of baleen. It was beautiful! Each of us took a picture of ourselves in front of the smiling whale so we could show the picture to friends and say, "Look at the whale I found!" Then, as the shadows were lengthening, the four of us got into the back of the truck and enjoyed the fresh air and unobstructed views as we wound our way down the hill, through a scenic canyon, and on through the fields and villages to the highway—a day to remember.

In one of the villages on the road we often took was a small, multi-purpose canal next to the highway. In the morning, women would wash their clothes there, and as we drove by in the evening, we might see men taking baths in the canal—sometimes skinny-dipping right next to the Pan-American Highway!

During the preceding week, Peru had declared a state of emergency because of the strikes and sent out the army to control the highways. When Ronny left to return to Italy, the taxi took him at four o'clock in the morning so that he would get to Lima before the strikes began. Our only emergency out in the wilderness was a flat tire on one of the trucks.

Sergio told us what to expect with Peruvian strikes. He said Peruvians like to argue with the government but that it was all for show. Peru doesn't generally have violence on such occasions, as often occurs in some other South American countries. The government sends out the army and stations big tanks in the city, and they make a lot of noise but don't fire one shot—it is mostly pretend.

It seems that in one aspect of Peruvian life, natural selection has been very active—dogs are everywhere. When we drove through the villages and farms, dogs chased our cars, and they were even abundant along the Pan-American Highway. Yet I saw only a couple of dead dogs along the road during our two months of travel. The only dogs around are the quick ones that had gotten car dodging down to a fine art.

We learned to appreciate Sergio's philosophy of life and the softness of his heart. One evening, Sergio went to town in Ica for a while and then returned and asked me for an advance on his salary. I gave him the one hundred dollars he asked for (a lot of money for him), and he returned to town. In town, he had found two young girls from Lomas huddled in a corner of the plaza, crying. They had come to Ica looking for work but hadn't found any and were out of money. After living in the street for a few days, they were cold, hungry, and scared. Sergio said he had watched these girls grow up during his many fossil hunting trips to Lomas, and it broke his heart to see them crying in the street.

Sergio spent the money on clothes and food for them and put them on a bus back to Lomas.

Sergio reads widely and has a practical, commonsense approach to life and people. I knew that I could trust a person who, while he was unemployed and had little, and knew that he could get tens of thousands of dollars on the black market for some of the fossils he found, he did not do it. He saved his fossils for the Lima Natural History Museum, which didn't even have the money to pay him for his work.

I also knew why Sergio had some fossils stored in a synagogue—his grandmother's name was Goldstein. When she and her family escaped from Germany, they dropped the Gold, and became Stein. When the local rabbi learned that Sergio was part Jewish, he had befriended Sergio and invited him to visit the synagogue.

Knowing Sergio also helped me to answer the question, "Who cares about fossil whales?" I believe that the important things in life all have to do with relationships—relationship with God or with other people. A friend once described an interview he saw on a TV talk show with a prominent actor. The actor was asked what makes a great lover, and he replied, "A great lover is someone who can bring happiness to one woman all her life." The important principle in his answer applies not only to marriage but also to other relationships—with our closest, most-loved friends and family, other friends, and strangers God brings into our path. The principle is that the greatest happiness and satisfaction in life comes from bringing joy and hope to another person.

But what does that have to with fossils? For me, everything. My research on fossil turtles in Wyoming and whales in Peru had been fascinating to me, but that was not why I did it. It had been hard, dirty work, and sometimes just plain lonely. My motivation is that doing this type of research, and doing it well, contributes to certain relationships. First, it helps to strengthen the faith of many people in God as Creator, because it helps them understand how fossils fit into the Bible story. In addition, many in the world are surprised that a creationist can do high-quality science, and their respect for the work brings opportunities for constructive friendships with them. I have been able to answer questions from atheist scientists about heaven and hell and about what salvation is—questions they would probably have never asked a pastor. Those opportunities are worth all the digging in the dirt after fossils!

Leonard Brand excavating whale IC41.

The trip was drawing to a close, and I thought about what we had discovered. After all our diligent work, we knew that not just the upper part of the Pisco Formation in Peru has well-preserved, articulated whales, but that they occur all the way down through the formation, almost to the bottom. This tells us that much of the Pisco Formation accumulated rapidly—but not all of it. Some intervals show evidence of enough time for colonies of oysters to grow on the rocks, along with small worms that made their calcareous tube homes in colonies on hard surfaces. It seems likely to us that this Miocene and Pliocene formation developed not during the biblical flood but in the turbulent centuries after the Flood.

We had finished the main part of our research, and it was time to go camping for a few days for the final phase of the work. We had been working mainly in a north-south chain of large Pisco Formation hills. Just west of those was a long field of very large sand dunes, up to two hundred feet high or more. We drove around the south end of the dune field to the valley of Corre Viento and on to Cerro Queso Grande (Big Cheese Hill). More whales were waiting to be excavated, and we had time to study another bed with zillions of fossil clams that might offer insights into how the Pisco Formation was formed. This clam bed was several inches thick—solid clams—and extended for miles in all directions. How had that happened?

Our camp at Cerro Queso Grande (Big Cheese Hill).

After that final phase of fieldwork, we were ready to return to Ica, and on Wednesday, our truck driver would take us to Lima. We would stay overnight at Sergio's friend's house and spend Thursday with Sergio at the museum, studying the fossils there. Then, in the middle of the night on Thursday, we would board the plane for Houston. Our collaborator, Tom, who had joined us for the last part of this trip, would be going to Chicago, and I would head for Los Angeles and home with my family and friends. I could stop counting the days.

At home, lots of work waited for me—the yard, for example—that had been neglected for two months. I planned to take some time off during the week to get the work done so my wife, Kim, would be able to relax and be ready for a very important event—our daughter's wedding.

16

SERGIO AND THE DEVIL

The trip was ending as it began—"Man plans, God laughs"—although I don't think He was laughing this time. Concerning our truck driver, Gilberto, we still didn't know if we were collaborating with the devil or not. On Sunday, we left for our last camping trip and stopped at an outdoor market to buy some groceries. Tom and I stayed by the truck and carefully guarded it while the rest went shopping. Then we drove more than an hour into the desert and prepared to excavate a huge whale.

When we arrived and prepared for work, Tom discovered his backpack was gone, containing his video camera, a digital still camera, passport, field notebook, and GPS—including valuable research data. We sadly made the trip back to Ica to file a police report. On the way, Gilberto said his brother-in-law worked for the Ica city government, and he would see if his brother-in-law could use his connections to try to recover our things. As we were unloading our truck at the Bendezu home, Gilberto also said he would talk to his contacts in the underworld to see if they could help recover the stolen things. (*He has contacts in the underworld?* I questioned in my mind.) He said we might have to give the thieves $350 to get our things back.

Two hours later, Gilberto returned with the news that our things had been found, and for $350 we could have them back. He had with him in his truck two very large men who looked like thugs, and we wondered why they were there.

A number of things were beginning to look suspicious. How did the thieves get that backpack while we were watching so closely? How did Gilberto know they would want $350? How did he find them so quickly, when there might be a number of thieves in Ica? We also knew, however, that we had no recourse but to play his game if we had any hope of getting our things back, or at least the most important thing—our research data. So we gave him $350 and waited.

After a few hours, Gilberto returned with one of his wives. (Sergio had accidentally discovered that Gilberto has two wives—one in Ica and one in Lima.) He didn't have the backpack and seemed extremely nervous as he reported that he had been set up and robbed. He returned our $350, which he said was from his own money. Sergio asked him how he could be robbed with those two big guys in his truck. Gilberto's reply was that they were just kids. Some kids! I would hate to meet those "kids" in a dark alley!

I remembered that a couple of people who knew Gilberto had said to us before that nobody would rob him.

While he was gone, we had been digging into our memories for details, and they began to fit together. Three of our group remembered seeing Gilberto at the market carrying a large black plastic bag, which we realized never appeared in the truck after the market stop. In addition, when we were driving back to town, Gilberto seemed to know in detail what was in the backpack. We became convinced that we knew who the thief was. It seemed likely that Gilberto had returned our $350 because he realized he had made too many mistakes and we would know he had stolen the bag. He was now trying to make himself look innocent—but without much success.

Sergio told Gilberto we had decided to do some work for our church the next day and that if we needed him to drive for us later, we would call him.

After Gilberto left, Sergio expounded in more detail his view of Gilberto, and we began to get a clearer picture. Gilberto had apparently been grooming us for this step for a long time. He had warned us several times to be careful to guard our wallets and other things, probably to prepare us to expect robbery attempts. Then our lunch container had disappeared from under our noses, and Sergio's suspicion was that Gilberto had arranged that job as well after he had increased our expectation that theft was a likely possibility.

Other recollections also helped to fill out the picture. Earlier in the summer, we had left Ica to spend a few days at UPeU in Lima, conducting a creationism symposium. We planned to take to Lima all the fossils Sergio had collected, including the beautiful, complete dolphin that Gilberto was so impressed with. However, Gilberto had refused to transport Sergio's fossils to Lima. He repeatedly said that he would need permits from the government office of transportation and other agencies before transporting the fossils. Sergio laughed at what he was saying because it was all nonsense. It was only illegal to sell the fossils or take them out of the country.

Sergio was a representative of the museum and had verbal permission to collect fossils, but he did not have a written permit with him. Gilberto knew this and seemed to be alluding to it. Sergio went with us to Lima and immediately asked the museum director to write out an official collecting permit. He returned early to Ica with his permit and "slept with his fossils" until we returned. It seemed to us that Gilberto was determined to prevent Sergio from taking his fossils from Ica.

Sergio then told us some other things we had not known. A couple of people in Ica were illegally collecting fossils and selling them, and Gilberto had been one of their drivers. He had been with us when Sergio was locating fossils in Corrie Viento the previous year, so Gilberto knew the location of those fossils. It looked as though Gilberto had taken the thieves to the places where they could steal fossils before Sergio could find the funds to collect them.

At this late point, we had already paid Gilberto in advance for the next week's work, including the final drive back to Lima, but we were no longer willing to work with him. We were beginning to be concerned for our safety as well as the safety of our possessions. We called one of our previous drivers, Felipe, and arranged for him to take us back to the whale the next morning for another try at excavating it.

When we were ready to leave in the morning, Gilberto showed up and angrily insisted that we had already contracted with him to be the driver, and he demanded that Felipe unload everything from his vehicle. Sergio spoke for us and told Gilberto that I had made the decision not to work with him anymore.

Gilberto said, "Do you think I stole your things?"

Sergio replied that it all looked very suspicious, and we didn't trust him anymore and did not want to work with him. Gilberto drove away, and we noticed that he drove ahead of us some distance and watched to see where we went.

With some concern, we went on to our two-day camping trip and the successful excavation of a beautiful, complete whale that also had baleen in its mouth. On that trip, Felipe told us of the clinching piece of evidence. A few days earlier, Gilberto had said to Felipe, "If the gringos lose their notebooks and cameras, do you think they will pay three hundred and fifty dollars to get them back?" That seemed to explain why Gilberto had tried so hard to keep Felipe from driving for us—Felipe knew too much.

On Tuesday evening, we got back to the Bendezu home and called our other part-time driver, Enrique. He agreed to come right away and take us and Sergio's fossils back to Lima during the night. We did that for several reasons. Large-scale labor strikes were in progress in Peru that would close down the highways in some places during the day, and we wished to get to Lima before the strikes began again in the morning. Also, Enrique and his assistant driver needed to go to work the next morning, and it would take four to five hours for the drive to Lima and the same to return.

The third reason for leaving quickly in the night was Sergio's concern that Gilberto could have more planned for us. From what we now knew about him, it was conceivable that his original plan had been something like this: by his extortion, he would get $350 for the return of the stolen goods and look like a hero for negotiating their return. Then, on the final trip back to Lima, the truck would be accosted at gunpoint, and our money, computers, and cameras would be stolen while Gilberto seemed to be a fellow victim of the attack. We did not know if that was in the plan, but we didn't wait to find out. We hustled ourselves, our equipment, and Sergio and his fossils back to Lima in the dark of night.

The fee for that trip was a bit high, but I didn't argue about it. On the trip to Lima, Sergio told Enrique about the theft, and Enrique revealed that Gilberto had also asked him what he thought the gringos would do to get their things back if they disappeared.

Our truck driver, Gilberto, in the days before he stole our things.

During this research trip, we had learned to appreciate Sergio not only for his excellent knowledge of vertebrate fossils and his uncanny ability to find them but also for his character and his understanding of people. He had become well acquainted with and understood the best and worst of Peruvian people. If he had told us earlier about some of his suspicions concerning Gilberto before the theft occurred, he could have seemed paranoid; but now that he was telling us what he thought, it all fit together.

He had never trusted Gilberto, and when Gilberto had used false reasons to keep us from taking Sergio's fossils to Lima earlier, Sergio realized that Gilberto was determined to keep those fossils in Ica, probably to frame Sergio and ruin him by complaining to the authorities that Sergio was collecting fossils without a permit and to accuse him of selling fossils. That was the reason Sergio had quickly gotten the written permit from Lima.

An event from the previous year seemed to fit into the overall picture at this point. Gilberto had been the driver for Raul Esperante and several others on a similar trip. One day, in the middle of the day, a group of government officials had appeared at the research site in the wilderness and asked to see the group's permits. This does not happen routinely in Peru. Those officials were tipped off by someone that they ought to make that specific trip to that specific place at that time. Gilberto did not know that Orlando Poma had a government research permit for the work and looked surprised when Orlando pulled out the permit. The most likely scenario was that Gilberto was hoping we would need to pay money to keep out of jail, and he could get a cut of those funds for tipping off the authorities.

We spent the night at the home of Sergio's friend Mike, and in the morning, Sergio said to Tom Goodwin, "Stop worrying about your belongings and eat your breakfast. Here in Peru, we fight or eat, but not both at the same time." We figured that was why the big labor strike and demonstration the day before had ended in the early afternoon—so the strikers could go home and eat!

At the market that morning, Sergio bought some donkey meat for his breakfast. I told him I felt sorry for the donkeys, and he replied, "Don't worry about the donkeys—they are old. When a donkey has finished his career, the farmer may sell him to the butcher." I later commented that I hoped the money he earned working for us would keep him supplied with tamales and donkey meat for a while. He replied that most of the money would be used to collect fossils and haul them back to the museum. He would hire local people to help him and to haul his fossils, and thus the money would be recycled to people poorer than he. That is a truly dedicated paleontologist and lover of people.

When Sergio had translated my final goodbyes to the Bendezu family, he translated my promise to see them in heaven but added his own comment, in English, that he wouldn't be there. I hoped that was not true, because it would be a sad day indeed if he isn't there. After arriving home in the United States, I had an opportunity to let him know that we would miss him if he isn't in heaven. A few weeks later, in an email, he told of many personal problems he was having and ended with, "Please pray for me."

We sat in the airport waiting for our flight to take us far away from Gilberto and his thugs. Sadly, it was also taking us away from such wonderful friends as Sergio and Mike, who had helped us a great deal. Besides everything Sergio had done to help us with paleontology, he was worth more than we paid him just for his knowledge of Peruvian culture and how to negotiate the rough spots. On future trips, we would know who to trust.

17

GOD HELPED YOU AGAIN!

The previous year's trip was not the last one after all, just as Sergio had said, and with memories of the difficulties in mind, we carefully followed Sergio's advice in planning for the next trip.

We arrived safely in Peru, and after spending the first night at UPeU, we picked up two rented pickups at a Toyota dealer. This seemed like the best vehicle rental we'd had on all our trips. We had two almost-new Toyota pickups with dual cab and four-wheel drive. We hoped for no more truck breakdowns and no more thieving drivers. Ah, the joy of a reliable vehicle that can take you anywhere! We would do our own driving. When we left the dealer, one of the employees said, "Good luck," which I presumed was a commentary on driving conditions in Peru.

Sergio joined us when we drove down to the fossil region. Our first bad news in the field was that someone had kidnapped Fernanda—our favorite whale, whose photo had appeared on the cover of *Geology*. Someone had dug her up and taken her away, and she would probably end up in someone's private collection. I had suspected this would happen sooner or later.

Each morning, I prayed for open eyes and an open mind to see what

God wanted us to learn with all these fossils. We were learning all the time and were eager to learn more. So many fascinating questions waited to be answered!

The first day was a "clam day" for me—following a layer full of zillions of fossil clams, checking our mapping from two years earlier, and correcting any mistakes before we published our research for all the world to see. The question was, Why were all those clams jammed together in one layer for mile after mile? All were articulated (the two halves of the shell closed), which meant they were buried alive, or within hours after death.

The delightful little ten-dollar-per-night hotel on the beach at Lomas, Peru.

Our plan this year was to double-check our stratigraphy around Ocucaje and near Lomas. As we followed marker beds in our research area to understand the stratigraphy, it was important to know if the rock layers were continuous or if they were broken and shifted by faults. On this day, in our research area near Ocucaje, we found a couple of faults that were hard to see, which we had missed in our research two years earlier. We corrected the mistakes in our stratigraphy that resulted from these faults.

The next day we would leave for the little fishing village of Lomas. I would be working with Sergio and his graduate student, Gerardo. Everyone in Lomas knows Sergio, so they would take good care of us.

When we arrived, we decided to skip the five-dollar-per-night hotel and check out the fancier one down the street. Built into the rocky hill by the beach, it had nicely tiled floors and patios, rooms with a beachfront view, and decent bathrooms (but still no water in the sinks). The price was ten dollars per night, which didn't leave much incentive to return to the five-dollar place we had stayed in last time. The hotel was owned and operated by a nice little old Peruvian woman named Pepita. For another six dollars a night, she fixed a special veggie dinner for me each evening. She fussed over that meal like an old mother hen. Sergio said all Peruvian mothers of her generation are like that. I wondered how she could make a living, since I was her only customer, except for a couple of old retired men who live there all the time. I found that she is actually wealthy and runs the hotel only because she wants something to do. Sergio and Gerardo stayed at the home of a friend—a woman who drove an oil truck. They were sad because the weather was too windy and the sea too rough for the fishermen, so there were no fish in the market.

We finished our work around Lomas sooner than we expected, partly because some of what I hoped to do really can`t be done, at least not in the time we had available, so we had to give up that part. We excavated a fossil cormorant and worked on the stratigraphic relationships of the locations near Lomas where Sergio and Gerardo were studying the fossil cormorants.

Late one afternoon during the work near Lomas, we were making one last stop way out in the wilderness to examine some fossil locations. We were driving down a gentle slope toward the ocean when the ground turned suddenly from a hard surface to soft sand, and we didn't notice it in time. The truck was seriously stuck. I pondered what it was going to be like sleeping in the truck.

We decided that since we were only about fifty feet into the sand, it would be better to drive backward up the gentle slope rather than forward, which would take us farther into the sand. While it looked as though we could go forward and turn to the right to get to firmer ground, turning in sand tends to bog you down even more. We worked for a couple of hours and made progress digging out of our deep hole in the sand and moving the truck back part of the way to solid ground.

However, as darkness was coming on, the three Peruvians with me decided we needed to give up on going backward and go forward instead, through the sand. They began letting the air out of the tires, since having the tires almost flat makes it much easier to drive through sand. I had a hard time accepting that, since we also had to drive a long way home after getting out of the sand. What if they let out too much? But they live there and know the desert, so I kept my mouth shut as they let out that precious air. They said, "Now we need to go forward." I sat in the truck, still keeping my mouth shut, with Sergio in the passenger seat urging me on. Going forward into the sand sea seemed like a do-or-die proposition—we would either get out, which seemed like a slim hope, or be hopelessly stuck in deeper sand.

Our truck seriously stuck in the soft sand, south of Lomas.

I sat for a few moments and pondered the options, but there weren't many options. It was getting cold, and we were far from anyplace with other humans. So I said out loud, "God, You will have to help us get out of here!" and charged forward into the unknown. We gathered momentum and began slowly turning to the right as we made our way toward solid ground again. We got out of the sand, and Sergio exclaimed, "God helped you again!" I rejoiced inside to hear him acknowledge it.

In the darkness, two of our group walked ahead to watch for soft sand as we found our way to our older tire tracks that could lead us out of the wilderness and back to the highway. When we got to it, a strip of asphalt never looked so good! Pepita was waiting at the hotel and worrying about us.

The next Sabbath afternoon, I saw penguins for the first time in the wild at a nature preserve by the ocean not far from Ica. We drove to a cliff about eighty feet high and sat at the top. From this vantage point, we could see the curving cliff and the rocks below. We saw many sea lions, three kinds of gulls, two kinds of cormorant, pelicans, blue-footed boobies (a large oceanic bird that dives into the water like a bullet to catch fish), and oystercatchers. It was fun to watch the flock of birds circling in front of us at eye level. Most exciting for me were the penguins. They were standing in a low cave, and they jumped into the water and swam—though it looked more like surfing—through the waves crashing against the rocks.

Earlier that morning, a few minutes before the church service, someone had asked me if I would preach. That was more warning than I'd had two years earlier in the same church. Thinking ahead of time that this might happen, I thought up a sermon before church (since I had already given my two prepared sermons there).

Anytime we drove past the farmers' homes outside of town, dogs would come running out and chase our trucks. At one place, two medium-sized, whitish dogs always took up the chase. One morning, they came after us, barking as usual. We were on a fairly smooth, straight stretch of the "road," so I pushed the pedal closer to the floor. The dog running outside my window stopped barking and, with an eager spirit, took up the challenge of the race. It seemed to be enjoying itself as it stretched its legs, and its lean body flowed over the ground like a graceful racehorse for quite a distance—a beautiful sight to watch. Its top speed that morning was forty-three kilometers per hour.

The research was going well and had become routine by now. It was interesting to watch Sergio as he prepared for a female graduate paleontology student from another South American country to come to spend a few days working with him and learning about his fossil dolphins. He did not want a female student to visit him in the field, because he didn't think a woman could take the difficult working conditions or adapt to living in the lowly village with its dirt-floor homes. He had told her so and tried to convince her not to come, but she was determined to come and didn't take well to being told that the field is no place for a woman.

I teased Sergio about this, and he was a good sport. It wasn't that he was not experienced relating to women—not at all. He said that he didn't want any women or children to complicate his life. He loved his fossil dolphins and penguins and said a woman would take all the excitement out of life because she wouldn't like such things as camping in the desert. I did notice that in the morning, he was clean-shaven and wearing the best field clothes I had ever seen him in. He grumbled that because of this woman, he had to take a bath.

One week that summer, we saw some fascinating fossils on a side trip. Sergio showed us a couple of fossil whales he had found in a rock formation that was older than the one we were studying. This type of whale, called an *archeocete*, is extinct and very ancient. These animals were quite different from our modern whales.

We were driving from one specimen to another when I saw a big, hot dog–shaped concretion. Concretions are masses of rock of various shapes that are more cemented together than the surrounding rock and remain together when the other rock around them erodes away. Some concretions form because the organic material in a dead animal or plant changes the chemistry of the sediment that buries it and turns it into harder rock. You might say the organisms make their own coffin. Inside these coffins can be anything from an insect to a mouse skull or even a whole large animal.

The big, hot dog–shaped concretion made me suspicious, and I said, "I would bet there is a whale in there." We drove on without stopping, but on the way back, we stopped and looked at it. Indeed, whale nasal bones were sticking out from one end and tail vertebrae from the other end. We then began looking around at numerous large, elongated concretions in the area, and each one contained either a whale or a tree trunk. Sergio's assessment of the day's work was, "We have found more archeocete whales today than in the whole history of South American paleontology!" To discover unique and rare specimens is exciting.

A common sight at the Bendezu home,
with our laundry on the clothesline.

The Bendezu family, with whom we were staying again in Ica, took excellent care of us. At one point, we were leaving for a more distant place than usual, so we left at 6:30 A.M. instead of our usual 8:00 A.M. The Bendezus were up at 3:00 A.M. cooking for our lunch. I felt guilty about it. We had never been able to convince them it wasn't necessary to do such things as iron our underwear, nor had we been able to get them to make simpler lunches that could be put together quickly. As a group, we were quite adaptable in the desert. On the latest trip to Lomas, we had plenty of bread and fruit and a few avocados and other things. The first day, we had avocado sandwiches. The second day, we had only one beat-up avocado left, so we had squishy avocado and vegetarian hot-dog sandwiches (not bad when you are hungry in the desert). By the third day, we were down to peanut butter and jelly sandwiches, but we were happy to eat them.

Our work in Peru was turning out to be more educational than we had anticipated. UPeU had begun a program in environmental science, including environmental geology, and Orlando Poma was a teacher in the program. That particular week, he brought nine of his students to work with us to learn basic geology. In addition, several of the theology faculty were spending a few days with us, learning more about whales, science, and how faith and science fit together.

Sergio and Craig, a graduate student in Lima, were developing an educational program to introduce the schoolchildren in the village of Ocucaje—near our fossil whales—to the field of paleontology. Sergio's friend wanted to be a high school teacher, and the two of them had a burden to improve the educational program for children of poor people in Peru. They developed science units for the schools, with printed material and slide presentations, using our whale research as examples for teaching science and especially paleontology. Craig took our geology publications and translated them into Spanish, written to a language level appropriate for schoolchildren. The two men began in Ocucaje and worked on getting their materials into the schools of the larger city of Ica, with its 40,000 high school students.

Sergio and Craig met with school officials, city officials, and senators to introduce their program. They were thinking big. They wanted to eventually make their learning modules available on the internet to all of South America.

The two were thinking of education but also economics. The exceptional fossils in that area could become a tourist attraction, a source of income for the local people, and they felt the need, first, to educate the people to appreciate and understand the fossils. Some people were determined to believe that the fossils were dinosaurs, not whales!

One such person, especially, was one of our suspects in the vandalism inflicted on some of the whales. Not only had they stolen Fernanda, but they had smashed some nice whale specimens that were already exposed on the ground surface, and it was hard to comprehend their reasons for this.

Finally, one more week and I could head for home. God had kept us safe, and it had been a productive trip. I learned more about Sergio on this trip. He had been, at one time, a wealthy businessman with an export business. He also said that he was in love with a beautiful woman (who is now a

Peruvian TV personality). He said, "They wouldn't let her marry me." I didn't know who "they" were or why they wouldn't let him marry her, and he didn't seem to want to talk about it. Possibly, it had something to do with his being part Jewish; he had said that Peruvians are more prejudiced toward Jews than even the Germans were. Whatever had happened, he didn't seem to hang on to any bitterness.

When the Shining Path guerillas had been active in Peru, they had spoiled his business, so he had left to work in another country for a while. Upon returning to Peru, he was introduced to fossils and fell in love with studying them. Since there was no employment for paleontologists in Peru, he gave up on women and on making money and had worked at a survival level with his fossils.

At the time of our trip, he was spending much time, money, and energy on his projects to help the education and economy of the village of Ocucaje. Partway through the summer, he asked me, "Will this be enough to get me into heaven?" Later, I tried to tell him what I think is involved in God's decision on such matters, and he replied, "I can't think about heaven—I have too many things to do for these poor people in Ocucaje. God can't take me yet."

Sergio also used much of his meager earnings to hire local people to help him. He didn't seem to know anything about theology, but his life reminded me of Matthew 25:40, where Jesus said, "Inasmuch as you did it to one of the least of these My brethren, you did it to Me" (NKJV).

18

BODYGUARDS AND FOSSIL THIEVES

D etails! Do we really have to concern ourselves with details? The Pisco Formation has the most abundant and beautifully preserved marine animal fossils anywhere in the world. But what about the details? After the previous year's research trip to Peru, I prepared a paper for a geological journal on the stratigraphy of the Pisco Formation. But some details seemed uncertain to me—especially the relationship between the lower units of the Pisco and the underlying Chilcatay Formation.

I could make a few guesses, and perhaps those would look good to almost every reader. Would that be good enough? The theologian Elton Trueblood had a good answer: "The religious scientist has more reason to be careful of his evidence than has the nonreligious scientist, because he is handling what is intrinsically sacred. Shoddiness, for him, is something to spurn because it is a form of blasphemy."[1] Therefore, we needed to deal with the details before proceeding with publication. That required another summer trip.

Kevin, Raul, and I, and students Jamey and Chelsea, arrived at the Lima airport at midnight and met Orlando and Edgar from UPeU. I knew we were back in Peru when we stopped for a red light in down-town Lima and the car next to us made a left turn from the right lane, crossing in front of us, against a red light—a local interpretation of the traffic "suggestions."

The next day, a car rental outlet had our fleet of three Toyota Hilux four-wheel-drive pickup trucks ready for us. The paperwork was all ready, and we were on our way by ten o'clock in the morning. *What is happening to Peru?* I wondered. The three trucks provided the independence we needed for Kevin to search for volcanic *tuffs* (distinct layers of air-distributed ash that fell over a wide area), for Raul and his students, Jamey and Chelsea, to study preservation of whalebone surface details in different ancient environments, and for me to pursue finishing the stratigraphic details, with Sergio's help.

Sergio, Raul, and two Peruvian helpers
with our three rented trucks.

We enjoyed a grand reunion with our friends, the Bendezu family, in whose house we again stayed. We settled in for three weeks of research and living with this charming family. The Bendezus don't have a steady income, but as is common for them, we found out, they were helping someone with needs greater than theirs, including boarding a relative and her child after her husband ran away.

One important difference set this trip apart from our previous ones—they had taken place in the Peruvian winter. Now it was summer, and hot—especially at night when we were trying to sleep. And in Lomas in summer, a lot of tourists crowd the beach. The makeshift restaurant set up there played loud music late into the night and began again at five thirty each morning.

Back at the more northern study area, near Ocucaje, we found some more whales—always more whales! And the whale with the big smile was still smiling! Sergio knew now who had stolen our favorite whale, Fernanda—a man named Jovani. He was not a black marketeer, only a troublesome quasi-scientist who thought he was the local expert and protector of all of Peru's fossils.

Compared with some other of our Peruvian trips, the logistics were fairly straightforward. Only once did one of us get stuck in the desert sand. We had no vehicle breakdowns except for two flat tires (Kevin), and we weren't robbed. Nevertheless, research is seldom uneventful. Some days brought futile searching in the penetrating heat or wind-blown desert sand, while others were satisfying days of finding the answers we sought.

As it turned out, the answer to the uncertainty about the base of the Pisco Formation is that it is uncertain. But now I knew that it was uncertain not because we had not looked enough but because there didn't seem to be a clear boundary between the sediments of the two formations—more of a gradual transition from one to the other. Now we could make that statement without apology. A clear boundary might someday be identified through new types of evidence, but the evidence available right then did not give us that certainty. The biggest difference is in the types of fossils in the two formations.

Kevin's volcanic tuffs had the potential to test my interpretation of the stratigraphy. If I was right, the tuffs he had found on the southern group of Pisco mountains would not be found on the northern mountains, because they would be below the ground surface. If he found them on all the mountains, then I would have to start from scratch on the stratigraphy. What would he find? I had no doubt in my own mind because I was confident in the work we had done. However, honest research can humble us sometimes. It can be beneficial for a scientist's maturity to have one of his pet theories destroyed per day!

At the rock outcroppings, we took photographs, collected more rock samples at the excavated whales, counted fossils in a couple more transects (study areas of known size, to determine fossil density), and finally, started to get blown off the slopes by the increasing wind and blowing dust.

On this short trip, the time seemed to be going fast, but we were finishing what we needed to do. We found a huge whale just begging to be excavated, so that would be our next task.

When we were leaving for this dig, Raul and Sergio tried to talk our host, Ephraim, into leaving an outside door of the house unlocked, or at least to leave the key somewhere accessible. Every outside door had a security door of iron bars, and Ephraim locked them at night and kept the key. No one could go in or out unless he unlocked the door, even in an emergency. He said, "What could happen? I will come and unlock the door." His wife laughed and said, "Do you know how long it takes him to get dressed and find his glasses?" They forget that the town of Ica had been destroyed at least three or four times by earthquakes, and the whole city of Lima was destroyed by an earthquake in 1647. If it started to shake while we were inside, I thought, we would have to help Ephraim find his glasses! I guess people are the same everywhere—we don't like to think there will ever be any trouble where we are.

A few months later, a significant earthquake did hit this area, causing serious destruction to Ica and nearby towns. The Bendezus' house came through without much damage, but the Adventist church we had attended and the adjacent church school were no longer useable and had to be rebuilt.

Sergio was in good spirits. He had recovered from a life-threatening infection in his jaw a few months earlier that had resulted in the replacement of most of his lower teeth. Now he could once again chew the donkey meat he liked. He was doing fine, even though he complained about the lack of chicken or ham in our meals. We told him the soup had chicken in it, but he wasn't very good at pretending.

He found some fascinating fossils on this trip: a penguin; a short-faced dolphin with one long narwhal-like tusk that extended downward from its upper jaw; an otter-like *protocetid* that is usually interpreted as an ancestor to whales; and others.

Collecting that protocetid was another adventure, as we were first accosted by Freddy Gonzalez, a guide who happened to drive by with a load of tourists on a tour of the desert. He tended to be a little confused about his role, and, like Jovani, thought he was the protector of all fossils (although he actually stole and sold them). Then, three armed men from a little isolated village beside the nearby Ica River showed up to see what we were doing. One of them, a serious-looking policeman from Lima, wrote down our license plate numbers, but the other two were friendly enough. We found out they were bodyguards for an extremely wealthy man who lived like a hermit in this isolated village and had the guards because of occasional attempts to kidnap him for his money. (Aren't riches grand!) By the time Sergio and his three Peruvian workers finished collecting the fossil, it was late, but since Freddy knew where it was, Sergio was not going to leave it there overnight. In the Peruvian wilderness, life was seldom boring, even though it was the most desolate and empty place I could imagine.

As we came to the end of our trip, I was thinking about the contrast between our vehicle experiences this year and our first Peru research trip in 1999. This year, we had picked up our new Toyota pickups—with insurance, comfortable seating for five, and air conditioning—in Lima and driven them to Ica and then to Lomas. Everything worked fine. We had learned the system of where to get reliable vehicles and how to stay safe, with Sergio's guidance. At the end of the trip, we would turn in the pickups after a perfect, comfortable driving experience.

The driving in 2007, compared with that of 1999, also seemed rather boring because we didn't need to exercise much faith, and we didn't have the inspiration of knowing that our angels were active in keeping us going day after day. So should we have continued renting that old Jeep

Cherokee in order to save money and experience continual reminders of God's care? I don't think so. To do so would no longer have represented faith but rather presumption—asking God to work miracles for us even though we now knew where to get reliable and safe vehicles. But does that mean that as we learn more, we need God less? Again, the answer is no. I believe that when we learn from our angels the full truth about our life experience in this dangerous place called earth, we will learn that the events of special, apparently miraculous care that we did see were only the tip of the iceberg of God's watchful care over us and His guidance in our lives. Should we expect God to continue changing our diapers when we are experienced enough to do better? In life, we learn how to deal with the challenges. Of course, in the really important area—our salvation from our sin-damaged existence—we will never escape the diaper stage until we experience God's transforming grace, when He comes to take us home. May that be soon!

The next day, we began the long trip home and all the duties awaiting us there. First would come the long drive to Lima. Then we would turn in our rental trucks and take a taxi to the museum for some observations of the fossils there. Then the midnight flight would take us back to family and friends and away from fascinating fossils, misguided bodyguards, fossil thieves, our wonderful Peruvian host family, our friend Sergio, and the desert heat and ever-present dust.

After the trip, I learned that Sergio was looking for specialists in the US and elsewhere to study various groups of his fossils. He was communicating with two European paleontologists about studying his seal fossils. One of them found out that we were creationists. The man was very upset about it and emailed Sergio to scold him severely for collaborating with creationists. He advised Sergio to stop working with us because "they will ruin your reputation." Sergio answered him and said, "They have their beliefs, and I don't care what they believe. In the field, they work like other scientists—and better. And they appreciate me more than anyone else does." Sergio removed the Europeans from his list of potential collaborators and continued looking for someone to study his seals.

One camera was stolen in the Lima airport as we left, but that was a small price to pay for the wonders of this rich Peruvian research adventure. It was at least as great as that valley full of dinosaurs I have dreamed about.

---

1. Elton Trueblood, *The Yoke of Christ and Other Sermons* (Cambridge, England: James Clarke Lutterworth, 2000), preface.

19

SCREENMEISTERS IN WYOMING

After an absence of several years, I returned to Wyoming with a research group after my trip to Peru in 2004. Five of us made the trip—Tom Goodwin, me, and three students. Ryan was in good spirits, even though his mother had incurable cancer at that time. Rahel was a married graduate student from Andrews University. And Erika was a student at Loma Linda Academy, a Christian high school. Erika was younger than most of the students we bring on these trips but was a valued and capable member of the team.

This year, we spent our time finding little fossils—hundreds of them—called microvertebrates. We did that by a process known as screen washing. First, we were "rock jocks," digging up rocks and filling five-gallon pails. We took the rocks to camp and soaked them in water to dissolve them. Dissolving rocks may sound strange, but while some rocks are "hard as rock," many others that are also called rocks are not solidly cemented—they do in fact dissolve in water. Next, we were "screenmeisters." We put the dissolved rock in a set of trays with screen bottoms of various-sized openings and used water pumped from the river to wash the sediment through the screens, leaving the little fossils and the undissolved pieces of sediment in the screens. Then last, we became "bone pickers," picking the fossils out from the bits of sediment (very tedious!). These little fossils provided evidence to help us figure out how the sediment along with the fossils got deposited in the first place.

Screen washing along the river, in the Bridger Formation.

Our camp was beside a peaceful, slow-moving river surrounded by aromatic sagebrush, clumps of scrubby trees, and impressive cliffs on the other side of the river formed of chocolate and vanilla layers of rock. Some wind had made everything in our camp very dusty.

The wildlife around camp and on our journeys along off-road trails was a continuous source of interest. In the morning, we woke up to the beautiful songs of meadowlarks and mournful dove calls. The night activities of mice, bushy-tailed woodrats, rabbits, and kangaroo rats always left many tracks. A rabbit lived in camp and often hopped around within a few feet of us. An eagle sometimes roosted on the cliff. One morning, five deer were feeding in the meadow across the river but were afraid of us. Imagine the day in heaven when we can walk together through the meadows, petting the rabbits and tickling the deer behind their ears!

In the morning, I would sit by the riverbank, watching the river drifting lazily by and the violet-green swallows cruising above it, listening to the meadowlarks, and communing with the Maker of it all.

We drove through the wilderness on off-road trails, with our trip interrupted a couple of times when we succumbed to the temptation to wait beside a prairie dog hole for the curious mammals to come up to peer at us. We saw a coyote and several bands of wild horses. On the way home, a band of ten wild horses, including two colts, began to run as we came toward them. They ran down a path approximately parallel to ours with a fluid grace that always fascinated me. They disappeared behind a hill, but as they came out on the other side, it was apparent their path was converging with ours.

Wild horses, a common sight in the hills
of the Bridger Formation, Wyoming.

One more hill, and they were even closer. Soon, they were galloping only twenty yards from us. I drove as fast as feasible on the off-road trail to keep us neck and neck with the thundering herd, while the others in my group snapped photos from the car windows. Such a beautiful sight! Then the horses passed us and ran ahead of us on the road. They didn't seem to be galloping all out but instead maintained a steady speed that the colts could handle. The colts began to tire, so we slowed down and let them go their way. This was the most glorious encounter with horses in all our years of research.

Our wildlife-viewing day was complete when we discovered a rattlesnake coiled up and resting under a bush in our camp. He didn't seem concerned about us, so we didn't worry about him. By the next morning he had left, and we didn't see him after that. I guess he found a less crowded neighborhood.

A woodrat by his nest on our truck engine.

Around our camp were some bushy-tailed woodrats. We normally would not see these attractive and fascinating creatures (they don't deserve the derogatory name *rat*), but they had been making unfortunate choices of homesites—in the truck engine compartment. They seemed to think that was an ideal site, which might say something about the shortage of good, natural homesites available there. We had not been able to discourage them, and when we drove away each morning, it seemed they stayed in the engine compartment for a while and then tried to leave by jumping down on the top of a tire. The result was a flattened rat on the road. We unwittingly killed at least seven of them that way.

When we got up each morning, one thing we often did was to check the animal tracks in camp, typically including woodrats, rabbits, and field mice. One morning, I got up earlier than anyone else and created a set of tracks through our "kitchen." I used the side of my fist to make the palm prints, and four fingers to make toe prints on the front of the palm prints. They looked convincing! When the others in the group got up, they were puzzling over the tracks—measuring them, photographing them, and comparing them with diagrams of tracks in the mammal book. Finally, I could keep a straight face no longer, so I made one more print for them, and they realized they had been taken in. Later, Ryan tried to get even by putting watermelon rinds behind my tent to attract the woodrats, but I outfoxed him because I discovered the rinds and moved them.

Our menu included breakfasts of such delights as cold cereal, instant oatmeal, toast, frozen waffles, and fruit. A couple of times, the women in camp made homestyle hash brown potatoes. At noon, we had sandwiches, and in the evening such things as spaghetti, vegetarian chili with peas or chopped veggie hot dogs, and vegetable soup. We wielded a mean can opener!

On Sabbath, we went to the little Adventist church in Rock Springs. We made up about one-third of the congregation while attending there. After a great potluck lunch, we spent the afternoon in the Uintah Mountains, ending the day with a picnic lunch by a lake and looking for beavers along a peaceful little stream meandering through a meadow. While we didn't see any beaver, it was a great Sabbath day.

Picture the scene when we were screenmeisters, washing sediment through screens to get the fossils. Three persons worked over the screens on the riverbank on a warm day, each with a water hose and nozzle in hand. As the sun rose higher in the sky, a temptation would begin and grow stronger as the heat increased. One Friday, Ryan, Erika, and I were screen washing, and suddenly, without warning, a water fight erupted. I didn't initiate it, but I didn't necessarily get the worst of it either. I will have to admit that I had been thinking this would be a good time for a water fight, but they beat me to it. A few days earlier, Ryan and I had been doing our duty as rock jocks, collecting samples, and Rahel was photographing Tom and Erika doing the screen washing. On a prearranged signal, Erika turned the hose on Tom, while Rahel photographed the scene for posterity.

One weekend, we drove up to the Wind River Mountains on a Friday and returned Sunday morning. At that beautiful location we camped in the campground at Green River Lake and, on Friday evening, sang many songs with guitar accompaniment from the three members of our group who played. We spent Sabbath on a hike to a group of alpine lakes overlooking the main range of high granite peaks. Along the trail was a wonderful patchwork of color from the wildflowers. Ryan and Erika found a snowbank and had a good snowball fight. We saw deer, many squirrels, and one moose.

A minor miracle occurred on the way back. It began to rain, so we were hurrying down the trail and had to walk across a couple of logs spanning sparkling, singing streams. A couple of us had gotten ahead of the others and finally stopped to let the others catch up. Ryan came up, carrying my camera. He had found it hanging on one of the logs where it had landed fer it had fallen out of my pack as I was crossing a stream. He said the log was mostly smooth, except for a couple of short branches sticking out. The camera strap had caught on one of the branches, and the camera was hanging a few inches above the rushing stream. Thank You, God, for the camera rescue! Psalm 121 ends with a beautiful promise: "The LORD will watch over your coming and going both now and forevermore" (NIV).

During the trip that year, several rainstorms came through, often with thunder and lightning. Most had brought only light rains, but on one Wednesday evening it was a downpour, and some of our tents got wet inside. Camping does build character! Then one evening a few days later, a storm brought rain and a fierce wind. Afterward, a rainbow arched across the sky, and a bright sun shone under the clouds and lighted up the cliffs behind the camp while the students sang and played their guitars—a beautiful memory after a hard day's work.

Our work this particular summer indicated that the small mammals, lizards, birds, and small fish were not preserved complete, as the turtle shells had been, but were instead the fragmentary and scattered remains of disarticulated carcasses. Why were they more fragmented than the turtles? Perhaps because small animals decay and fall apart much faster than turtle shells and are easily scattered by flowing water. Or possibly the small animals were already dead and disarticulated before the episode of volcanic eruptions killed the turtles. Our field data didn't tell us the answer. Rahel would study the thousands of little fossils in the lab for her master's thesis, and we were happy to see her tackle the task of finishing the solution of this puzzle.

The work was interesting and profitable, and the research group was a pleasure to work with, but I thought often of going home to see my family and friends again. The time passed quickly, and it would be great to be home again. I now had enough fingers to count the remaining days.

We spent one evening visiting the research camp of geologist Paul Buchheim, near Fossil Butte National Monument. We left as a blazing sunset was spreading across the western sky. Soon, the scene grew more interesting as two sage grouse sauntered onto the road in front of us. We didn't see them often, and they were interesting birds. Then we noticed an owl hovering in place, riding the updrafts along the hilltop. It seemed intent on something on the ground. All of this combined into a fascinating scene on the sagebrush and pine tree–covered hilltops.

The fifteen-hour trip home from Wyoming, down Interstate 15, was uneventful. I didn't know how remarkable that was until the next day. I emptied the chuck wagon trailer and was towing it home to clean it when I drove over a small bump, and suddenly I heard a racket and a scraping noise. I looked in the mirror and at first couldn't figure out what I was seeing—it was the front of the trailer pointing up in the air. The trailer has two metal beams that go from the hitch to the trailer and are welded to the bottom of the trailer. These had apparently experienced metal fatigue through the years, and they had finally both broken almost all the way through, right at the front of the trailer. Only the bottom of each beam was not yet broken, and now they had bent so that the back of the trailer was dragging on the ground. I moved all remaining weight in the trailer to the front, lifted the trailer back into its proper position, and very gingerly drove it to the university campus engineering department for repairs.

Why had the trailer held together through rough wilderness driving and through the long trip home, mostly in the midst of highway traffic, and then broken from hitting a tiny bump two blocks from home? I just thank the Lord for keeping us from what could have been a serious and destructive accident.

(20)

NEW QUESTIONS AND RATTLESNAKES IN UTAH

The plans for my next project and our research trip in 2007 were all made—I would meet three fellow researchers at the Las Vegas airport on a Wednesday morning and drive the remaining three hundred miles out into the wilderness of west-central Utah for two weeks of research. Then someone from the airline called and informed us that they had canceled the early morning flight from Tulsa because of bad weather in Dallas, and one of our group would arrive at eleven thirty at night instead of ten o'clock in the morning. My pleading and begging didn't help—all the other flights were filled.

We finally accepted the revised schedule and settled into a couple of rooms in a motel until the next morning. So far, things were as expected—that is, not going as planned. In addition, I would not have expected to be delighted at buying gasoline for $2.65 a gallon, but that was the price in Cedar City, Utah. It was $3.65 in Baker, California, at the cheapest station in town.

This new research adventure would be in the desert mountains of the House Range, Confusion Range, and the Wah Wah Mountains—an area of dry but ruggedly charming rocks, sagebrush, and patches of juniper trees. It reminded us that the earth is shattered and broken, the ruins of a drowned planet, but there is still beauty among the rocky ruins. We found a delightful campsite in a group of juniper trees beside a picturesque whitish quartzite (metamorphosed sandstone) hillside. After setting up the chuck wagon and situating the portable latrine behind a large juniper tree far from camp (you have never seen facilities with such a view as this one had!), we headed for the first research location.

The chuck wagon at our campsite in
the House Range in western Utah.

Some scientists are precise and organized in the way they plan research. They like to read about their topic and know, before they begin, the questions they will ask and just what types of data will answer the questions. In my own paleontology research, that approach often doesn't seem to work, but my concept of the research unfolds as the initial phase of the work proceeds. To plan our basic research goals and read the research literature ahead of time is necessary, but I need to be in the field and get my hands dirty before I know what specific questions to ask and what data will answer the questions. This seems to result partly from my habit of independent thought and partly because my understanding of earth history is not the same as that of many scientists. If a person accepts the conventional worldview of earth and biological history, with its millions of years of evolution, that concept limits the questions to be asked and may even influence which answers will be acceptable. Many of my questions are different and arise from my biblical worldview, and thus they could not derive directly from the published scientific literature. I need to see what the rocks have to offer before I know what questions are going to bring the most insight. Before beginning the day's work, my prayer is, "Open my eyes so I can see what is really there."

We were in Utah, and it was time to confront the puzzles hidden in the rocks. Our thoughts were a confused mixture. We had been looking forward to this opportunity to begin directly seeking to understand how the rocks relate to the biblical story of the Flood, but how would we know what we were doing there? We were eager to challenge the secrets of the history of these rocks and fossils, but none of us were experienced with the Paleozoic (the lowest third of the fossil record). We had the chance to ask new questions and make new discoveries, but because no one has ever seen a worldwide geologic catastrophe, how could anyone figure out how to relate the rocks to the Bible story of earth history? The task we had chosen seemed hopeless, impossible, but when we take God with us, we cannot fail to accomplish His will. So it was time to get on with the job.

The quartet working together on this project was a challenging combination. One was quite conservative in his views on origins and firmly believed that almost all the rocks were formed in the one year of the Flood. Another was almost as conservative, and the two of them were not sure about my ideas that some of the rocks and fossils might have formed between Creation and the Flood. The fourth had more uncertainties than all of us and wasn't sure about such conservative ideas, but our differing viewpoints balanced each other out, which helped to keep us from being careless. We were all friends, committed to the Bible and willing to think new thoughts and to question the conventional scientific viewpoint. If we questioned that conventional viewpoint, we couldn't allow our own bias to dictate the result. We would have to trust that an honest understanding would emerge with the aid of solid scientific work. I expected we would have a great time working together.

We each had our contribution to make. One of the group wasn't healthy enough for vigorous fieldwork, but he knew a lot about paleontology and could come up with twelve new ideas before the rest of us had two. And there was a good chance that one or two would be ideas we needed. Another of the group sometimes wanted to do more than we could realistically do, but he worked hard and knew more sedimentology than the rest of us. The third might focus on details sooner than some thought we should, but he was a careful-thinking scientist and made a valuable contribution. My role was as the generalist who knew how to get things done and bring people together for the project, and who was also too persistent (the proper word is *stubborn*) to give up.

One of the delightful little antelope ground squirrels
eating our sunflower seeds in the House Range, Utah.

One afternoon we were going through a geological section up a hillside that had been thoroughly studied by another team of geologists. The previous group had measured sections in a number of places and painted numbers on the rocks along their sections. We could follow the numbers and know exactly where we were in their measured sections. This was in a place called Lawson Cove, in the Wah Wah Mountains, and all the rock there was limestone, full of microscopic fossils called *conodonts*. If other geologists had already studied it, why were we studying it again? We did so because their careful, thorough work and well-written research papers helped us get acquainted with these limestones and prepared us to think of those new questions.

Back at camp, we enjoyed spaghetti and a salad of peas and cucumber, and then we prepared for the night. Have you ever tried a peas and cucumber salad? If not, you should!

In the cool of the evening, it was very quiet. We noticed that while we were gone during the day, some little antelope ground squirrels had made a shambles of the big trash bag that hangs at the front of the chuck wagon. But they were so cute that it was impossible to be mad at them. We found it necessary also to be careful of the rattlesnake that lived between camp and the juniper tree comfort station.

The antelope ground squirrels used our
wastewater bucket as their water source.

At my home, our family always had ice cream on Friday night to begin our Sabbath. So to keep up the tradition in camp, our Friday evening meal was finished with a surprise of pumpkin pie and ice cream, then songs with a guitar, and finally, a long, peaceful sleep. The next morning, we learned that the Great Basin National Park wasn't far away, so we packed a lunch and made our way to the pine forests of the park. A short hike to some awesome three-thousand-year-old bristlecone pine trees and an inspiring alpine lake was a welcome contrast to the dry desert.

The multiple layers of limestone we studied in the House Range, Utah.

Saturday night, we sat in camp and brainstormed about what to do next. One idea had been stewing in our minds the previous couple of days. The limestones we were studying had been interpreted as accumulating gradually over millions of years as the ocean level rose and fell in cycles—called Milankovitch cycles—related to climate change. If, as we believed, it had been a much shorter time since Creation, these cycles of tens or hundreds of thousands of years couldn't be real. We had known for years that this theory needed to be challenged and tested—could we find a way to do that? Was that the reason we were out here? Another explanation must exist for the monotonous repetition of layers of limestone, each between a foot and several feet thick. Was each layer an event—perhaps a lime mudflow—instead of a long cycle of sea-level change? One way to test that could be to study the taphonomy of the conodonts to see if they were distributed in each layer in a way best explained by the mudflow hypothesis. Would that work? Was that the insight we had come there to find? Or was it just a stepping-stone to some better idea? (Science often works that way.) We would only know after collecting samples and having them analyzed. In any case, we had our research plan for the next few days.

A few days later, the day had been spent in more exploration of the local geology and in further development of our plan. Now I needed to take Lee to the airport, while the others examined a hillside across the valley from camp—a hillside that was, as Lee would say, chucky-jam-packed with fossils.

We spent the next day climbing back up the marked section in the Wah Wahs and collecting rock samples. We collected a sample from the top, middle, and lower parts of each layer. We would send these to a lab to dissolve the limestone in weak acid to release the conodonts. Then we could study conodont taphonomy, including the distribution of conodonts through the rock layers. The rock was very hard, and the collecting was difficult, but we secured our cargo—just ugly old rocks to most people but precious to us.

After the next Friday afternoon town trip, our camp life had been livened up with a bag of sunflower seeds. We hadn't changed our diet, but the local animal population loved them! The largest count of antelope ground squirrels in camp at one time was twenty-three, plus a chipmunk, a lizard, and some doves. The lizard and doves didn't eat the seeds but seemed to enjoy the party.

One morning we noticed a flock of chukars (a type of quail) in the rocks behind camp. The squirrels were also coming from some distance around—how did they spread the word so fast? They knew where the food was coming from. When I appeared at the feeding area with the bag of seeds, they quickly gathered in front of me, looking at me, running nervously back and forth, and chirping as I tantalized them a bit. Such charming creatures the Creator gave us!

Numerous fossil brachiopods in the limestone
at Fossil Mountain in the House Range.

The past few days had been filled with more rock-sample collecting and exploration of other possible research projects for the future. Then on Sabbath morning, we were close witnesses of one of nature's dramas, and it began with pancakes. We were peacefully enjoying a delicious breakfast of pancakes topped with peanut butter, applesauce, and fresh strawberries and blueberries from our refrigerator. I turned from the cookstove just in time to see a three-foot rattlesnake crawl out from under the breakfast table, where my two colleagues—unsuspecting pancake-munchers—were eating!

The snake's track revealed that he had come from under a nearby bush and crawled right under our chairs, before heading for the squirrel feeding area. He situated himself under the shaded edge of a large rock, right in the middle of a snake banquet of tasty squirrels. In his eagerness, he struck unsuccessfully at a couple of squirrels. Then he settled in to wait, as the foolish squirrels frequently came to within a foot or two of him, watching him and stamping their back feet and waving their tails back and forth in their indication of stress or curiosity. Why did they taunt him by approaching so close?

It seemed they could assess his position and know how close they could come, and yet stay just beyond his striking range. Perhaps the snake's strategy was to sit and wait while the squirrels became progressively less cautious. (Isn't that the way the devil works?) In the early afternoon, we left for Great Basin National Park again, so we didn't see the end of the drama. I am betting that before the day ended, at least one squirrel was missing in action.

One of the rattlesnakes we had to be careful to avoid.

While we were dodging rattlesnakes, my cell phone was accumulating messages from home that a couple of sprinkler systems had stopped working and that another wouldn't stop running and was sending a stream of water down the driveway. Some law of nature must be behind those things happening when I am away from home!

We broke camp and headed for civilization one day early for several reasons. It had been a productive, satisfying trip, and we had a lot of good material to work on at home. One tire on our car was destroyed by rock damage, and thus we didn't have a spare tire. It was getting hotter each day and was currently 103 degrees Fahrenheit. Last, we were out of cans of Hansen's soda. There's nothing quite like ending a long, hot day of fieldwork by sitting in the shade of the chuck wagon awning with a cold Hansen's right out of the refrigerator.

The time had arrived to analyze our samples and get expert help from those more experienced in the Paleozoic, to be sure we hadn't made foolish mistakes. We had come to Utah with many questions and uncertainty about just what we would do and how to be sure it would be a productive trip. The answers to our questions still awaited the results of the lab work, but the Creator of the universe had a plan for our lives and for His work, and we could trust His plan. He would lead us to the secrets of the rocks in the way, and at the time, that He knows is best. Our part was to keep looking, keep doing careful work, and keep trusting His leadership.

21

LEARNING TO TRUST GOD'S GUIDANCE

At the end of a one-week intensive course I taught in Nigeria in 2008, I had two days to get home and prepare for a three-week research trip to Utah. The two days were an exercise in learning to trust even more that God knows how our problems will be solved and remembering that to stress over them won't help.

Chiemela Ikonne, my Nigerian host, suggested we leave for the Lagos airport by 3:00 P.M., even though my flight was not scheduled to depart until 10:00 P.M. Normally, it would be a one- to two-hour drive, but things can go wrong. We actually left at 3:30 P.M. with an expert driver who knew the city and highways well.

Traffic was flowing smoothly on the expressway—for a while. Then the heavy traffic came to a dead standstill. The driver knew this problem would not end soon, so he headed off to a country highway to bypass the traffic jam. Other drivers had the same idea, and we all carefully threaded our way through the abundant potholes. And don't think of these potholes as little nuisances—they were ten to twenty feet across, and a car could almost get stuck in some of them. After a time of 10 mph driving, we reached another expressway. Driving went well for a time, until again it reached a standstill. The reason was that southbound traffic had taken over some of our northbound lanes rather than deal with the heavy traffic on the southbound lanes. It seemed as though the traffic "suggestions" here were taken even more lightly than in Peru!

We reached the airport at 10:00 P.M., just in time to see my plane take off for Frankfurt, Germany. The airline agent rebooked me for the same 10:00 P.M. flight the next day, and for a flight from Frankfurt to Los Angeles. The next day at the airport, the airline agent informed me that my flight from Frankfurt was not confirmed—I was on standby. He was not helpful, and I was puzzled as to why he was hesitant even to give me my boarding pass out of Nigeria. While I pondered the nagging suspicion that he wanted a bribe, the younger agent next to him took my papers and helped get me on my way. I don't know if he was more honest or if he could see this American didn't know how to negotiate the system.

I was finally on my way, but the problem wasn't solved. I was still on standby in Frankfurt, and because it was the height of the tourist season, all flights were booked for the next two weeks. In Frankfurt, the agent confirmed that I was on a waiting list for the flight, and all flights were booked. I understood that citizens of Frankfurt are called *frankfurters*, and it appeared that I would be a frustrated frankfurter for an unknown length of time.

Now, let me fill in the rest of the picture. This was mid-morning, I was on standby in Frankfurt, and the very next morning, six people would be arriving at the Las Vegas, Nevada, airport and waiting for me to drive them to our research site in the Utah wilderness.

I rehearsed Dr. Ikonne's advice: You are on God's business; He knows what will be the solution to these problems, and worrying about it will change nothing. Praying is in another category from worrying, of course, and I did pray. I also asked the agent if a possibility existed of finding other flights to Los Angeles, even if they cost quite a bit more. She recommended that I wait to see what would happen with my scheduled flight, and if I didn't get on, I could look for other flights.

As take-off time approached, I noticed ten or twelve other people waiting around, presumably also on the waiting list. What were my chances? How would I get in touch with the others who would soon fly to Las Vegas, and even if I did reach them, what would I tell them? "But don't stress," I told myself. "It won't help." (It's a good theory!)

Minutes before closing the door of the plane, the agent called me over and gave me a boarding pass. Was there rejoicing in Frankfurt that day? You bet!

The Lufthansa boarding pass that finally allowed me to
leave Frankfurt, Germany, and return to California.

Carl, one of our student research assistants, was waiting in Loma Linda to ride with me to Utah (with his box of live rattlesnakes). In the few hours remaining after I arrived home, Carl helped with food purchases and other preparations for the three-week trip. I didn't forget anything important except for my sleeping bag and pillow. Fortunately, Utah was kind to me—the nights were warm that first week until I could get to town and buy another sleeping bag.

Our scenic camp among the junipers, against a backdrop of white quartzite rock, soon became a pleasant home for the group of three paleontology professors and six students. After we had a morning session planning our strategy, the first stop was Lawson Cove in the Wah Wah Mountains. There, we collected more limestone samples for the study of conodonts, the tiny fossils with a toothlike structure. In addition, the portable gas-powered rock saw served us well for cutting out a pillar of limestone from the top to the bottom of a three-foot-thick limestone unit. To understand how such a layer of limestone was formed, it is necessary to study not only fossils but also the details of the rock itself. This cut sample would be further cut and polished for a study of the interior structures of the limestone.

We arrived in Utah this time with our research goals still somewhat vague. We were on an exploratory mission, based on the conviction that if we diligently searched, God would bring to our attention evidence to help us better understand earth history. But even as we trusted that plan, there was still the urgency of knowing that we needed to have some solid results to get another grant for the next year's research. As the one responsible for securing grant money, I felt that urgency.

Our campsite in the House Range of Utah.

Just below our sampling area was a large section of limestone we had briefly pondered the previous year. It had many circular or polygonal features several inches in diameter that previous researchers had called stromatolites. The reason they warranted pondering is that stromatolites are dome-like structures that form underwater by living cyanobacteria that trap sediment in sticky tendrils, adding layer after layer on top of the growing domes. Our reason for being there was to seek an understanding of how these Ordovician rocks fit into the biblical story of earth history. Were they formed in a few days or weeks in the Genesis flood? Or were they formed during the hundreds of years before the Flood? How could we know that? It would help to know if these were indeed stromatolites because each layer of stromatolites would take several years to form, and there are many layers of them in the Wah Wahs.

Our prayer each morning was not for proof of our pet theory about the rocks but simply for open eyes to see what was really there. These features didn't seem to have the types of internal laminated structure of real stromatolites I had seen before, so what could they be? Some details within them looked like the result of movement of uncemented sediment after it was deposited, rather than biological structures formed on the seafloor. The answer would come after laboratory analysis of the samples we collected. Another piece of the puzzle was on the table for study.

Contemplating stone circles on the hilltop needed to be followed by carrying heavy rock samples down the hill to the Chevy Suburban, but the students were ready for the task. This year's students were an interesting group—from Michigan, Tennessee, California, and Brazil. They ranged from those with enthusiastic Christian experiences to some struggling with many questions. When we arrived at camp, Maria, the organized list-maker, prepared the meal and planned our camp cooking and cleanup schedule. Evening saw us relaxing, reading, or watching ground squirrels gathering sunflower seeds.

The religious interactions between these levelheaded students were constructive for all of us. To hear their conversations was a joy. And when Carl left our group early to take his box of rattlesnakes home to Tennessee, the other students missed him. As one student put it, "I feel safe when Carl is here because I know just where all the rattlesnakes are." His box held one more rattlesnake than before—one he caught right in our camp.

It seemed that we needed a break from analyzing and collecting rocks, so we spent a day hunting trilobites at a commercial fossil quarry and a couple of other old quarries. The fascination of trilobites kept everyone as busy as if they were seeking gold nuggets. The day held a couple of surprises for us, however. The first surprise came at a quarry on the side of a hill. A thunderstorm came up, and we kept track of the distance to lightning strikes, which were not far from us. The storm was hazardous because the lightning was not accompanied by enough rain to make a difference if lightning were to ignite the dry bushes and grass. Several extensive brush fires begun by lightning were already burning elsewhere in the region.

After one loud thunderbolt, we noticed a column of smoke in a nearby draw. In a few minutes, the Suburban took us to a juniper tree blazing hotly in the midst of a small grove. We helped the students as they expertly attacked the fire with shovels of dirt and with wet towels, and by stripping off the burning bark with rock hammers. I wondered where they had learned to fight forest fires. Gusts of wind kept the fire flaring up again, so we didn't dare leave. We had the fire out by the time two four-wheel-drive fire trucks arrived to mop up the scene.

The time came for the journey back to camp and the second surprise of the day. A long stretch of smooth, straight dirt road followed along the flank of a range of hills, allowing for 60 mph speed in the Suburban. The road went up and down through a series of washes coming from the side of those hills. It was fun driving over the hills and dips, and one of the washes was deep enough to give us a little buzz, like a diminutive roller coaster, as we had made our way northbound on this road in the morning. On the southbound journey back to camp, we learned that this particular rise was asymmetrical in shape, because when we went over the top this time, the Suburban actually left the ground momentarily. The students were happy as they enjoyed this brief and unexpected Magic Mountain ride. I, too, was quite surprised.

Friday afternoon found us on the seventy-mile drive to town, where there were real showers, a laundromat, grocery stores, and a choice of restaurants to finish off a productive week. Then, in the evening, back at camp, the guitar came out, and we ushered in the Sabbath with the rejoicing of enthusiastic young and older voices praising God together.

A few days later, the time came for a trial run of a research technique we were anxious to try. I had been hoping for several years to try this approach. Our goal was to measure geologic sections through the geological column in Utah. Geologists are aware that measuring sections has been a standard research technique for a couple of hundred years, so why did we think this was new? That question can be answered with a little background information.

Measuring a section involves measuring the thickness of each rock layer, one above the other, up a hillside, and describing the characteristics of each layer and its fossils. In this instance, the only new feature of our measured sections was the questions we were asking as we collected data. A researcher never collects all the data that could potentially be recorded, simply because most geological phenomena are much too complex for that, and many possible observations seem irrelevant to the research. We tend to notice and record the features that have the potential to answer our specific questions. The questions a geologist or paleontologist is likely to ask are, in turn, influenced by their worldview. So we were asking, How long did we think the geological history has extended? We were well aware of such phenomena as radiometric dating and our lack of explanation for that evidence, but we were willing to wait for answers to those difficult questions while examining other types of evidence.

Other questions were these: Did the fossils record the result of large-scale evolution through the ages? Or is the Bible story of origins in Genesis to be taken literally? Since I answer the latter question with a yes, it opens the way for me also to ask whether most of the geological column was formed in the one year of the biblical flood, or were parts of it formed before or after the Flood.

This last question was the one we were addressing with our measured sections, so we were concentrating on recording data with the potential to indicate which parts of the geological record could have formed in days or weeks (during the Flood) and which parts of the sedimentary rocks seem to require years or decades or more (before or after the Flood). Essentially, no one besides creationists measures geological sections with the goal of answering this question. Thus, the geological features we systematically noted were chosen for their potential to answer this intriguing question. Would this method yield insightful data? Was it practical? Could enough data be collected in a realistic time frame?

Three of our team documenting bioturbation
in the Mancos Formation in Utah.

After three days of measuring sections, we decided the answer to all three questions was yes, and the data we recorded was consistent with a biblical time frame for these rocks. This work would be a featured part of future trips to Utah. Devising exciting new questions is, of course, only the beginning. We could not afford to be careless in this research. The biblical insights could lead us to ask the right questions, but then we needed to follow up with careful, solid science if we were to honor God with high-quality work. If we do sloppy work, God doesn't need our help.

Finally, the last data sets were recorded in our rainproof notebooks, several hundred pounds of labeled rock samples were packed in the trailer, and another fascinating research experience was becoming a memory. The students said they had appreciated the experience and the biblical values that guided the work. I was hoping the highlight of the trip for our students might be some great discovery we made, or perhaps finding a beautiful trilobite, or even perhaps that they would be impressed with the wisdom of their scientist mentors. But alas, when Paul, another geologist, visited our camp the last two days of the trip, the first thing they were eager to tell him was the moment when, on the road back to the campsite, the southbound Suburban had caught air!

22

BEDDED ROCKS AND FLYING SAUCERS

The following year, 2009, we returned to southern Utah. Art Chadwick, who had recently completed PhD study in geology in addition to his PhD in biology, joined a student and me on this trip to measure sections and count fossil worm burrows.

Do worms really make holes in rocks? The holes were made by animals burrowing through sand and mud before it was cemented to form rock. Many such fossil invertebrate animal burrows can be found in rocks. These burrows pose an important question for our research.

In today's world—in lakes and on the ocean floor—animals continually burrow through the sediment and obliterate any evidence of distinct layers of sediment. If rocks contain distinct layers not blurred by burrowing (bioturbation), does that mean not enough time may have passed for animals to make many burrows before the next layers were deposited?

We were back to the task of measuring sections through geological formations. In a previous season, we tried this process and decided it had the potential to yield useful data on the nature of many rock formations and on how much time they require for their formation. In these first efforts, we were concentrating on the abundance and nature of animal burrows and on how sharp and well-preserved the contacts between layers or beds of sediment are. These could help us understand how much time was required to deposit the sedimentary rocks.

Densely packed invertebrate burrows (bioturbation)
in the Hermit Sandstone in Arizona.

The first task was to find places where the rocks have clearly exposed surfaces that are not weathered enough to destroy the evidence we need to see—evidence of whether or not they have been extensively burrowed. We made a long drive from Las Vegas, across southern Arizona to Monument Valley, and then north to the San Juan River. The river flows in the bottom of a deep, precipitous canyon. That may not sound like a promising place for research, but its steep walls can be reached by hiking down the Honaker Trail.

After hiking down the trail and eating lunch by the river, we began the slow climb, measuring and examining the rock walls all the way to the top. Though the day was long, we left with considerable data, and there weren't many burrows in these Pennsylvanian rocks. In some places, the rock face was covered with soil, and we could not determine whether burrows were

present. This is often a problem in this type of work. Where could we find
better research sites? I decided that we would need to come back, climb
that trail again, and try for a more complete set of data.

Leonard Brand on the Honaker Trail in southern Utah.

Farther northwest, after crossing Lake Powell on the ferry, we found
some marvelous sheer cliffs in Mesozoic formations along the east side
of Capitol Reef National Park. This work was in early May, and setting
up tents in the RV park—with a cold wind whistling around us and
occasional raindrops—was almost more than we had bargained for. We
lost our enthusiasm for the canned food waiting in our chuck wagon and
found a little restaurant serving Mexican food. It turned out to be a poor
excuse for Mexican food, and we repented of our unfaithfulness to the
chuck wagon. And in weather like this, we would go through many cups
of hot chocolate!

I remembered that we had seen a series of steep hillsides in colorful

Triassic rocks farther south, near the Arizona border. We traveled back there, searched along these hillsides, and found the ideal site. At the base of a high mesa, the Moenkopi Formation sits on top of Permian Kaibab Limestone, and a road has been cut into the side of the steep slope, all the way to the top of the mesa. The flat mesa top is formed by the Shinarump Conglomerate, a hard rock that doesn't erode easily, which accounts for its flatness over a large geographic region. The hard rock cap also explains the presence of a high, steep cliff. The conglomerate protected the mesa from being eroded away. A road cut into a steep hillside like this one often results in fresh rock surfaces—wonderful for our work.

This mesa has a research facility building on its top, with an airstrip and a long test track. Fences and warning signs completely surround it, generating a bit of mystery about the place. Persistent local rumors have it that the site was at one time used by the US Air Force for developing a working flying saucer. The facility is still in use, and an employee on his way home from the test site stopped and spoke to us. He said the site is used for testing ejection seats. Was that all? Or was that the story in use to divert attention and decrease the mystery? On our long journey up the road, examining beautiful rock exposures that had resulted from the road construction, we entertained ourselves by making up stories about what was really going on up on the mesa. The road cut yielded high-quality data.

The sedimentary beds in that area are generally sharply divided from one another and undisturbed by burrows, with only minor exceptions. In places, there are horizontal burrows, and sometimes some vertical burrows, but not enough to disturb the distinct bedding in the rocks. At least some burrows can be found in many sedimentary rock formations, and some places are heavily burrowed. But thus far in our systematic search, most of the sediments did not have significant burrowing. In questionable cases, we took samples for examination under black light in the lab, which can show fossil burrows otherwise hard to see.

Putting rocks aside for a few moments, we found bumbleberry pie in Springdale, at the western entrance to Zion National Park. We weren't so busy with animal burrows that we couldn't stop for a meal that ended with bumbleberry pie!

Persistently bedded rocks—usually not significantly disrupted by burrowing—were characteristic of a surprising amount of the rocks we were examining. In today's world, new sediment layers deposited in water are soon disrupted and mixed by burrowing creatures. Why didn't that happen more often in the ancient sediments? Some burrows can be seen, and fossil animals should have made plenty of burrows (before they became fossils). In some cases, it is possible that the water lacked oxygen, keeping animals out. But would that situation persist for hundreds or thousands of years? In many cases, it seemed there wasn't enough time for organisms to do much burrowing. Only occasionally did we find heavily burrowed rock. The evidence seemed to show that these layered rocks formed quickly, not gradually over millions of years.

Art Chadwick and a student examining the clearly bedded rocks that should not have survived normal bioturbation, located at Kanab, Utah.

About a week later, we made our way back to the Ordovician limestones of western Utah. The addition of Ronny Nalin to our research group that year, joining Art Chadwick and me, held the promise of strengthening our efforts. Most of Ronny's doctoral dissertation was on limestones of the Italian region. After completing his education in geology, he continued his research on limestones, and the work in Utah was in his area of expertise. God had sent the right person at the right time.

We met Ronny and two students at the Las Vegas airport and headed out to camp several hours to the north. Setting up tents in the gathering darkness under our favorite juniper trees, we savored the transition from the noise of the ever-present slot machines at the airport to the solitude of camp in the wilderness. Under the protective gaze of Fossil Mountain across the valley, we settled in for another geological adventure.

There are certain structures in the limestone that we wished to understand, and the existing interpretations didn't seem convincing. Even when working in a biblical worldview, we didn't need to be afraid of the rocks, of research data, because what we were seeking is the true explanation of these features—an explanation that will stand up to rigorous logical examination.

We spent our first days in further study at previous research sites with interesting names, at Lawson Cove in the Wah Wah Mountains and at Sneakover Pass. We continued our examination of the limestones, collecting rock samples and taking copious field notes. As we loaded the chuck wagon trailer with rock samples, I wondered about the chuck wagon tires. Would they make it home with this heavy load of rocks? That is a perennial question on trips.

In the evening, some of Ronny's other talents came into play. His Italian heritage led to a spaghetti supper such as none we had ever experienced in a wilderness camp before. None of those bottled spaghetti sauces would do. We had the best sauce—made from scratch with handpicked, fresh ingredients—added to choice spaghetti cooked to perfection! We then understood the joke: "There are no more living Italians—they have all pasta way."

After allowing time for the spaghetti to settle, we enjoyed a game of three-can pick. It's doubtful you have ever heard of this game, which was invented by Loma Linda University geologists. The goal is to throw rock hammers (also called geo picks) at a line of three empty cans and earn points by knocking them over. The game became ever so much more fun with Ronny's entertaining running commentary all the way through. We also found it humorous that Ronny had never before heard of Italian dressing, which is an American invention.

More bedded rocks, located in the Summerville Formation, Utah.

The first week in camp, a very practical issue held us in suspense for a while. We had arrived in that part of Utah on Sunday and headed out from the last town with a full tank of gasoline. Each day, we drove the twenty-five miles from camp to the research site and back. As the week progressed, I watched the gas gauge in our Suburban, and it seemed that we would make it without taking an extra 140-mile round trip to town to fill the tank. But then we had to make an extra, unplanned trip back to camp to pick up some research items.

On Thursday, I began to wonder about that gasoline supply. We drove more slowly to conserve gas, as the gauge showed not much more than an eighth of a tank. We put the remaining fuel from a gasoline can into the car, but it wasn't much. On Friday morning, we left for our study site, prepared for a morning of research and then the weekly trip to town for showers and groceries. That morning in our devotional time, we prayed not only for open eyes to find the evidence we needed but also for our gasoline supply.

We headed out optimistically, watching the gas gauge carefully. When we left the research area for the remaining fifty miles to town, the gauge didn't look hopeful. It had an eighth of a tank left, and the previous evening, with just a little over that amount, the gauge had moved too fast for comfort on the trip to camp. I drove slowly, watching the gauge closely and fearing the worst. This road was not a place where one can call AAA for roadside assistance. As we drove, I was amazed and grateful for what I saw. On the entire fifty miles of the journey, that gauge did not budge even a little bit until we were close to town. To me, that cannot be accounted for by chance.

The research on limestones was beginning to yield intriguing clues, but I realized it would take a couple more years before we could reach confident conclusions and be ready for publication. Research worthy of an honest Christian scientist cannot be done hastily.

Our research trips had been adventuresome, but the most exciting part was the new insights that resulted when we opened our eyes to see things in a new way, not bound by standard, unbending, modern, naturalistic scientific assumptions. We would not have discovered these fascinating insights in Arizona, Wyoming, Peru, and Utah if we hadn't actively questioned those assumptions.

$$\text{(23)}$$

TAKE TO THE AIR

C*an I really do this? Will I be able to pull it off successfully? Maybe I should have been more cautious about applying for a grant to do it! I have never done this before, it will cost a lot of money, and I don't have the time to do a short trial run first. It will all have to happen correctly the first time. All these things have to merge: all persons involved be available at the same time; good weather; and find the right charter company, the right equipment, and the right photographer at the right time; and I can't get sick in the process. This leaves some big questions for a challenging plan!*

These thoughts ran through my head as I contemplated my next research project. The plan seemed simple enough—several days of aerial still and video photography over southern Utah, from a helicopter, to document Utah's awesome geology. This footage would be valuable for collecting unique research data and preparing a film to share what we were doing in our research. But would it all fit together within the time frame of the grant I had for funding the project? I can handle stress pretty well, but the uncertainties were still there to keep one from being complacent.

I learned several important things as we proceeded. My first assumption was that we would need to settle for using an airplane because chartering a helicopter would be much too expensive. At the prompting of a friend, I checked out the alternatives and found there wasn't much difference in cost. First breakthrough! A helicopter would be much more fitting for this project.

Art Chadwick owned the right still camera for the job, but could I find an experienced video photographer to work with me? The answer came from an unexpected source. An expert camera crew from Loma Linda University had briefly joined a geology tour I led the previous summer to document that trip. In discussions with the group, they indicated a willingness to send a videographer on my new venture. Second miracle!

About the helicopter—the logical thing was to look online for Utah helicopter charters. I found several, but how would I decide which one was best? One website looked good, so I contacted the helicopter company, called FlyRight. *Certainly can't go wrong with FlyRight*, I thought. Initial email conversations dealt with which helicopter would be best for the job and how many persons would be in the crew. I envisioned the FlyRight people in their Utah headquarters in St. George or Salt Lake City with a variety of helicopters waiting on the pavement outside for me to choose from. It turned out, however, that reserving a chopper required a contract with them based on a specific flight plan. Having been on many geology trips in Utah and northern Arizona, I found it easy to picture in my mind a helicopter trip looking for the best geological features and viewpoints to photograph. However, the company wanted a specific flight plan. Out of all the possibilities, which would be the best locations to photograph? What time of day would the sunlight show each canyon and cliff to the best advantage? Which side of the chopper would the photographers be on? What would be an efficient route to fit all this together?

Working on that task was actually a fascinating puzzle to solve, but time was moving. Meanwhile, communication with FlyRight didn't seem to be proceeding well. Then they asked a new question: Did I have the permits to fly over the places I wished to go? That added more complexity to the puzzle. Some checking indicated that gaining a permit to fly over the

Grand Canyon was very unlikely, but how about the other places? Would this stall the plan?

FlyRight suggested a person who could help me with permits, M. J. Albertson. It took some valuable time to make contact with Mr. Albertson, but when I did, he was eager to help. He heard my vision of FlyRight in its Utah offices surrounded by helicopters and helped me understand it was incorrect. These people were in their office in Louisiana, working as an agent to match clients with helicopter companies for a fee. He said it would be cheaper to work directly with a helicopter company and suggested several companies. He also was very knowledgeable about permits and where we would or would not need them.

Of the possible helicopter companies, one was clearly in the best location for our plan, near St. George, Utah, the base for our trip. I made a phone call and learned that the pilot, Robert Joseki, knew all the places we needed to fly and was eager to work with us on our photography adventure—another breakthrough. Of course, I still didn't know much about him, but Robert and his company, Eagleflight Helicopters, seemed like our best option.

The next task was to find the right time for the trip. I hoped for mid-July, but then someone raised a new issue. June and July are the monsoon season in Utah—rain and lightning in storms coming from the south. How could we fit our plan into that? Another call to Robert, and he said he was not concerned about the monsoon rains. At that season the weather is great for flying from about six o'clock in the morning until one or two o'clock in the afternoon. Then it is time to stop to avoid the storms. So July it would be.

As the time approached, our video photographer, Cosmin, asked whether I had a camera gyro lined up. A gyroscopic camera stabilization system is very important for keeping the video camera steady during flight. FlyRight had indicated that a camera gyro comes with the helicopter. It turned out this isn't right—I would have to arrange separately to rent one. More searching online located a company and its distributors. One distributor is located in Las Vegas, not far from St. George. They had a stabilizer for rent, and it was available for the week of our trip. Another puzzle piece in place!

Then when the stabilizer rental contract arrived for my signature, it indicated one more puzzle piece I didn't know about. I had to provide an insurance policy to cover liability for it, and from a company acceptable to the rental outfit. Apparently, they didn't want to be responsible if we dropped the unit on someone's head from the helicopter. More online searching produced insurance companies that provide this type of coverage, for another significant fee.

The last issue that arose raised my discomfort level much higher. The battery for the unit lasts for three hours before needing to be recharged, and our flights would last up to five hours each. I couldn't find a backup battery, and the trip was rapidly approaching. We would just have to find our way through that one.

The beautiful Navajo Sandstone in Arizona, one of the formations we photographed from a helicopter. This is also where Leonard visited with Gary, the geology professor (chapter 24).

Some remaining questions still rattled around in my head as an inexperienced flier. I am somewhat sensitive to motion sickness. How would this affect me? What would it be like to sit in a helicopter for five hours with no doors between us and the sky? Had I correctly estimated the time needed for each site to be photographed? I trusted in the judgment of our pilot and told him we would be looking to his experience to help us work out the details of our flight plan. Trusting this to a pilot familiar with Utah terrain eased some of my concerns.

Leonard Brand with the chartered helicopter.

Finally, the day came to meet Art Chadwick and a geology student at the Las Vegas airport. We spent the first week in geology research in the St. George area, exploring the contact between the Moenkopi Formation and the Shinarump Conglomerate. According to the standard geological timescale, the mudstones of the Moenkopi Formation were deposited and then ten to fifteen million years passed before the Shinarump sand and pebbles were put in place, on top of the Moenkopi, by braided streams that found their way across an area of more than 100,000 square miles. Is that a realistic theory? We found evidence that makes it difficult to believe that any significant amount of time passed before the Shinarump arrived to cover the Moenkopi.

Finally, Monday morning arrived—the big day—and Cosmin and I met our pilot and his helicopter at the airport. We would soon learn whether all the planning had been adequate. After we heard Robert's careful instructions, we lifted off for the great adventure. We were sitting in a small helicopter with no doors. I had to regularly remind myself that the wind was moving six inches from my right elbow at 120 miles per hour. *Don't stick your arm out!* A previous client of Robert's had forgotten to keep his arm inside, and he needed surgical repair of his shoulder. After the first day, I was comfortable enough to enjoy the flight without leaning in, away from the great outdoors.

The uplifted rock formations along the
San Rafael Swell in Utah, from the helicopter.

As the week of flying progressed, we learned more about our pilot, Robert. He knew southern Utah like most of us know our own house. He had flown with firefighting crews, taken reseeding flights over burned-over areas with his helicopter, transported dinosaur-bone hunters to and from their dig sites, and had done a lot of wildlife work. This included counting wildlife from a helicopter, including elk, deer, bison, and wild horses in Utah and Colorado. This had clearly increased his skill at maneuvering his chopper. In some of the places we went, there was no helicopter fuel available to keep it in the air for so many hours, but Robert had the answer. A fuel truck followed, meeting us at crucial refueling stops. His team had obviously done this before, as the timing seemed to work out just right.

We became very comfortable with Robert's skill in flying a helicopter. The flights were surprisingly smooth and steady in spite of the wind that rises along many cliffs. He also understood how to adapt our flight pattern to the needs of a photographer, and his suggestions for altering our flight plans increased our efficiency in accomplishing our photographic goals. We found ways to stretch the Minigyro's battery life to accommodate these plans. It was going so well that the stresses of my planning were melting into the past. He also knew the laws governing where we could fly and where not to fly, with a sensitivity to avoid irritating any tourists who want a quiet wilderness experience. And frankly, the places he could fly were often more awesome than the tourist spots we needed to avoid. If we were to do this again, we would know just who to contact and how to plan the trip.

The helicopter on top of Lampstand Butte in the Circle Cliffs, Utah.

In spite of all this skill and comfort level, I still felt a strange feeling when looking out the open door into several thousand feet of nothing, down to the rocks below! Yes, the seat belt and shoulder harness are securely fastened, and there is really no reason for concern. The head knows what is true, but the feelings don't always get the message. Fortunately, we were frequently quite close to the ground, and the comfort level was higher down there.

Our photography had been planned with a couple of goals in mind. We would fly for many miles along some cliffs, documenting the rock units making up the cliffs. This would provide material to guide research on how these sedimentary layers were formed. The other main goal was gathering a file of dramatic views of awesome geological features for use in educating our students and for making a film portraying our research. The camera and Minigyro worked perfectly, resulting in smooth film footage in spite of the best efforts of the wind in moving the helicopter around. We learned much about the value of a helicopter in geology research. The planning next time would be much simpler and less stressful.

Although the project went smoothly, at the end I found myself bone-weary from the concentration and constant search for the next photo op. I was also somewhat dehydrated from trying to avoid unnecessary helicopter landings in the wilderness. Finally the trips were done, the questions answered, and another great research trip was history.

Our great God blessed our efforts to accomplish His purpose for us. Together with Him, we did it!

24

"YOU DO HAVE A DIFFERENT SEARCH IMAGE"

P lease, Lord, that's enough for today. I can't handle any more blessings in one day!"

That silent prayer came at the end of a day in the field with a geologist friend. The history leading up to it took several years to come about.

I had found evidence that contradicted the usual, conventional interpretation of a sandstone in Arizona—the Coconino SS—and published it. Gary, a geology professor at a state university, had called me with some questions about my interpretation of the sandstone. He didn't think my hypothesis that the sand was deposited underwater was a good idea and called to probe my thinking on the subject. It seemed that he really wanted to know if I had evidence for my ideas or if I was just trying to prove the Flood. The conversation was pleasant enough, but I was not able to convince him to put the sand underwater.

Through the following years, Gary and I continued to take different opinions on the origin of the sandstone. He argued that the fossil animal tracks I found could have been walking sideways without being underwater. I politely disagreed and explained that animals alive today never walk that way.

Some years went by, and one fall, I was attending the annual meetings of the Geological Society of America. The meetings are huge, with more than five thousand geologists and paleontologists of all types in attendance. These are always fruitful times to catch up on the latest research in any field of earth science you may wish to hear about. Sometimes, the conference even has sessions on creation and evolution, and these sessions are clearly not designed to encourage creationists. On the contrary, their goal is to combat creationism.

Leonard Brand and two students in the House Range, Utah.

Listening to research papers is not all that happens at scientific meetings. Some of the most important events are conversations in the hallways or at lunch with colleagues, where we hear about each other's lives as well as about research. We build friendships, learn firsthand about some fantastic finding, or begin research collaborations that lead to success stories. God can use these friendships to accomplish His purposes.

I ran into Gary, and we talked about geological things. He ended by saying, "I still don't know how to explain your fossil trackways." I appreciated his candid and non-argumentative comment and replied, "And I still don't know how to explain some of your evidence in the sandstones either." We left it at that, but his openness made me think I would like to visit more with him and discuss issues of common interest. I was quite sure he was not at all open to my ideas about Creation and a global flood, but he was not antagonistic about his views.

Later, I sent an email to Gary and asked if he would come to Loma Linda University to give a talk on some of his research at our department research seminar. He replied that he would be happy to do so, and we agreed on a date for the seminar talk. At the seminar, he talked about fascinating research on sandstones in South America and the fossils found there. In the afternoon, Elaine, another geologist, and I took Gary to the Los Angeles Natural History Museum. After the museum trip, Gary began asking questions. He said, "I know there is something different about the way you folks relate science and religion, and I would like to know more about it." That initiated a long, candid conversation. We told him the whole story about how we accept the Bible story of the beginnings of life and how we use that worldview to suggest hypotheses for geological research. We talked about the fact that our approach does not focus on disproving the standard geological interpretations but allows a biblical worldview to open our eyes to see things that we might otherwise overlook.

Some scientists would have shot back with incredulous sarcasm at our "naïve ideas" and made clear where we had missed the boat. Gary didn't agree with us but also didn't respond with condescending remarks. He was polite and gracious through this unique conversation and continued asking questions to learn more. The next day, he flew home, and it was clear that we parted as good friends.

The next fall, I was again at the annual geology meetings and again saw Gary. After a few greetings, he said, "I continue to be intrigued at how you relate science and faith." This encouraged me to pursue the matter further, so a few weeks later, I sent him an email asking if he would be interested in meeting me at my research area to examine the rocks and fossils together. He said he would—and so we did.

The next summer, we met at the "Roadkill Cafe" in a little desert town. After lunch (no roadkill on our plates), we headed out to a likely spot to find sandstone with fossil tracks. We went through a gate into a vast extent of sagebrush—cattle-grazing country—and up a winding wash to an area with plenty of sandstone surfaces exposed in the hillsides. We looked at the sandstone, and I showed him the best trackways I had found anywhere, including some that go sideways, in a way that animals are not supposed to walk.

Gary spent a few hours searching the rocks for the types of evidence that would tell him these sandstones were deposited in deserts. These features were not as clear in the Coconino SS as in other formations he had studied. That evening, we left the wash and drove to the Grand Canyon. I suggested we reserve a campsite for two nights, but he preferred to reserve it for one night and leave our options open for the next night.

The Roadkill Café in Seligman, Arizona.

In the morning, with lunches and plenty of water in our packs, we hiked down to the high, white cliffs of Coconino SS. What adventures would this day bring, here in the midst of so many questions about tracks and sand-stone? Gary again spent considerable time examining the specific features of the stone. At noon, we found a juniper tree with abundant shade and broke out our lunches (still no roadkill). Our conversation didn't stop with lunch, however. Gary had many questions. What is salvation? What are heaven and hell? Does a person have to belong to a particular church to be saved? I did my best to explain my views on these topics. He explained that he was once a Christian. He was not against religion, but when he studied evolution in college, he realized that Christianity was not true. His questions continued, and my answers sought to make my thoughts clear.

After a productive day in the canyon, we decided to leave and drive to a place where there were great exposures of the Navajo Sandstone—another cross-bedded sandstone—also interpreted as the result of migrating desert sand dunes frozen through time into beautiful, massive, red-sculpted rock monuments amid the sagebrush. In the Navajo Sandstone we examined features that looked very much like modern sand dunes, although there is an area that was thoroughly burrowed, while it was still soft sand, by some type of small creatures. Are there desert invertebrate animals that will make such extensive burrows in the sand? Some differences exist between the Coconino SS and the Navajo SS. Could one be a desert deposit and the other an underwater sand accumulation? Some of these questions are still waiting for answers.

We spent more hours in the shade of a tree considering answers to those other questions—the meaning of life and of the future. Gary tried to convince me that life is meaningful even if there isn't an afterlife. Was he really trying to convince me, or to convince himself? I wondered.

Our next stop was Coral Pink Sand Dunes State Park, with extensive modern sand dunes shifting with the wind. We examined the similarities and differences between these active sand dunes and the sandstones, frozen in time, that we had been examining. As the afternoon wore on, we turned toward the nearby campground. We had finished what we came for, and if I left now, I could be home that night. This time, however, Gary didn't argue for keeping our options open. He urged that we find a campsite and offered to pay for the site. He was eager to stay rather than head for home, so I agreed. But I wondered why he was so anxious to do so.

Watch for rocks! That is what we do on all our research trips.

The evening was spent in conversation, with the topic often on religious and philosophical subjects. Gary asked the questions, and I gave my answers to his questions. I am quite sure he would not have asked these questions of a pastor, but as fellow scientists, we had built a relationship of confidence that fostered an openness to probe each other's thinking on subjects of importance. An atheist and a believer in a Creator-God, we were a seemingly unlikely combination for fruitful conversation. But we had each come to trust the other's competence in science, apparently with a resulting trust that reached beyond science.

Gary still didn't know how to explain my fossils, and I still had unanswered questions about his sandstones. But he recognized that my approach to research caused me sometimes to notice different things than he noticed. I had discovered an unusual sedimentary structure in the Coconino SS. It had the potential to help us understand how the sandstone formed, and it had never been described in the research literature. His comment about my approach was, "You do have a different search image. I would have said 'That's odd,' and gone on."

The evening passed, and we each finally headed for our tents. I planned to leave early the next morning, so we said goodbye. It had been a rewarding few days of meaningful time with this searching gentleman geologist. As I crawled into my sleeping bag, my prayer was, "Please, Lord, that's enough for today. I can't handle any more blessings in one day!"

25

A VISION FOR THE FUTURE

T his summer, should I pursue the burrowed sediment research or the Coconino sandstone research? Well, why not both? And Art works his Wyoming dinosaur quarry Dino Dig in June, so shall we do our research in May or in July? Why not both?

These were my thoughts as I planned the next phase of fieldwork in 2012. I decided I had better be sure the yard sprinklers at my house were working well because it was going to be a long summer. So many fascinating puzzles waited to be put together, so why not go full speed ahead to find what new discoveries would open up? There were more hills to climb, more data to collect, and more papers to publish. All of this kept us coming back year after year.

Through the years, I had developed a way of describing the roles of faith and science in our understanding of earth history, which goes something like this. A discipline called epistemology is the study of how we get new ideas, evaluate knowledge, and decide what is true. It seems as if this should be easy—we carefully find the facts, and then we know what is true. But along the way we find pitfalls. Someday, when the opportunity comes, you can ask Adam and Eve about that!

Data, interpretations, and worldviews are all involved in the search for trustworthy knowledge. We collect a lot of data in our research. These are specific observations of things, such as fossil animal burrows in the rocks, or fossil whale bones in the desert. We record where they are, how many of them, and how big they are. Those facts are *data*, and they are just numbers and words on a notebook page, rock samples, or photographs in our computers. What we really want to know is, *What do they mean?* What story do they tell about the history of the rocks? In other words, how can they be interpreted? Data by itself almost never tells us directly what the interpretation should be, just as jigsaw puzzle pieces in a thousand-piece puzzle don't fall into place by themselves. We have to figure out how they fit together.

If we have a picture showing what the finished jigsaw puzzle will look like, the picture guides us in knowing approximately where the pieces should go. However, if we have the wrong picture to start with, we may arrange the pieces in a way that seems logical and may look promising, but we will have difficulty fitting the pieces together because our picture misled us at the beginning, and we have the pieces in the wrong places.

The puzzle picture can be compared to a scientist's theory, which guides in the interpretation of data. If he or she is convinced the rocks are a record of sediment accumulation and gradual evolution of life over many millions of years, that theory is the picture that will guide the person's attempts to understand and interpret data. If the scientist is studying, for example, the Morrison Formation, with its dinosaur fossils, the *data* will include a description of each fossil and where it was found. The sediments and fossils will typically be interpreted as an accumulation over a long period of time. That interpretation fits the picture provided by the theory. But is that interpretation correct? Conclusions in science always involve both *data* (specific observations and measurements) and *interpretation* of what those data are telling us—how they can be explained. Interpretations are strongly influenced by the theory (the puzzle picture) that inspired them to begin with and are only as correct as that theory.

In addition, an important difference between a thousand-piece puzzle and science is that in science, we never have all of the thousand pieces to work with. We begin with a few puzzle pieces (data, evidence) and gradually find more pieces, but many pieces are not available. Our interpretations are an attempt to make sense of the evidence we have—to arrange the pieces so the emerging picture makes sense. Our tentative arrangements of the existing pieces help us decide where to look for more puzzle pieces (more evidence) to fill in the blank spaces. In parts of the puzzle, we may find enough pieces so we can try to fit the interlocking edges of the pieces together, to test whether our ideas are right. In science, accumulating evidence increases the possibility of knowing whether these interpretations are correct.

In geology and paleontology, the problem of missing puzzle pieces is more pronounced because we are examining the ancient past. If we study the physiology of rabbits, we have rabbits that are alive *now*, right in front of our eyes, and can be studied in detail, with ever-improving methods of observing how their physiological systems work. In contrast, in the study of rocks and fossils, we cannot go back in time to see what actually happened. We do the best we can with the indirect evidence available. To seek the correct history of the earth and its life is fascinating detective work, but it has unique challenges beyond those in some other areas of research.

Data, interpretations, and missing puzzle pieces can only be adequately understood if we consider worldviews and how they influence our search for truth. As I've said already, a worldview is a set of assumptions that influences how we view the world and how we answer the important questions of life—such as where we came from, how we should live, and where we are going. Whether we realize it or not, everyone has a worldview, and how we interpret the evidence around us is influenced by that worldview.

At least some of those assumptions behind our worldview must be taken on faith, and they can influence just about everything. One worldview is based on the assumption that God is real, that He has communicated with us in the Bible, and that His communication can be trusted to give us truth. Another worldview assumes that no supernatural, miraculous events have ever occurred in the history of the universe and that everything must be explained by known or knowable natural laws. These worldviews certainly involve evidence, as well as faith, but how could anyone prove that no supernatural events have ever occurred? Or how could we prove the nature of God? An important element of faith always exists.

The following table presents two examples of worldviews, Christianity and naturalism:

	Christianity *The Great Controversy* *Between Christ and Satan*	Naturalism
Assumption	God is real and is the Creator of the universe and life.	The universe and life arose through natural law; no intelligent, supernatural intervention has ever occurred in the universe.
Resulting worldview	• Creation of a perfect, sinless world • Fall of humanity—bringing sin, evil, pain, and death • Redemption through Jesus • Future—restoration of sinless perfection to come at Second Coming	• All plants and animals evolved from a common ancestor • This evolution took many millions of years • Pain, suffering, death, and natural evil are normal, inevitable processes • Future—annihilation

We can broaden our analogy of the puzzle and let the puzzle picture represent a worldview. The concept applies in the same way as before. The puzzle picture (our worldview) guides us in interpreting data. If we accept the naturalistic picture, we will "see" the earth gradually changing over hundreds of millions of years, while life evolves. We see rivers, streams, and ocean currents depositing sediment during long ages of time, and in some places we see wind forming desert sand dunes. We will "see" these processes occurring essentially as they do today.

No room exists in this picture for God to be directly involved in history—to perform actions we call miracles—or for a global geological catastrophe such as the biblical flood. Scientists working within this world-view will always interpret the evidence in a way that fits this naturalistic picture. They "know" how long it all took, and evidence incompatible with that picture will probably not be noticed.

I work in a Bible-based worldview, and it provides a very different puzzle picture. In this picture, we see the earth created as a carefully engineered home for living things. Evolutionary change in animals and plants has been limited to microevolution and speciation within created groups. Organisms do adapt to changing conditions, but entirely new kinds of organisms don't arise by evolution.

At some point, the earth's geological balance was disrupted, and a global geological catastrophe resulted. The crust of the earth was destroyed, and many geological formations accumulated rapidly, as unusual water and wind (usually water) currents quickly deposited sediments, with their fossils. This was a complex process, with continents moving—sometimes rising, other times sinking. Ocean floors also rose and fell. Brief times of calm occurred amid the storms. On the surface it seemed chaotic, but even violent storms can deposit very well-defined, systematic series of sediment layers under the water.

Finally, the process slowed, and over a period of perhaps a few centuries, the last portion of sediments (much of the Cenozoic?) was deposited and then partly eroded away, as the earth gradually reached a new equilibrium. Then, in the final part of the picture, we see today's river and ocean systems depositing sediment on the smaller scale familiar to us now on our more stable earth.

These two pictures, or worldviews, are very different, yet they share many common elements, just as two puzzle pictures could be similar but with specific differences. Features in specific sediments indicate whether they were deposited in fast-flowing water or in standing water, which way the current was moving, and whether they formed on continents or in the ocean. And many more of these similarities are available for any geologist or paleontologist to use to interpret the evidence. The biggest difference is time—did this happen over millions of years, or in thousands of years?

As we examine the rocks, our worldview has a powerful influence over what we notice. So many details are available for us to measure and take notes on, but only some things will seem important. If we already "know" that geological history occupied millions of years, our interpretations will have to be consistent with that. We would probably not notice features that are not compatible with that worldview. Could it be that a firm commitment to a millions-of-years worldview will bias the interpretations?

How about the biblical worldview, with only thousands of years? Could that also bias one's interpretations? It could. The point to remember here is that whether we are aware of it or not, everyone has a worldview, and *any* worldview could bias scientific interpretations. The puzzle picture we are looking at will influence, or even limit, how we try to fit the pieces together.

So what is the solution to this dilemma?

For the Christian paleontologists I have worked with, it isn't really a dilemma. The solution is that we must be aware of both of the puzzle pictures and seek for evidence that could show whether one is right and the other is wrong. We don't allow a naturalistic, millions-of-years picture to control what we see in the rocks. We also cannot look only for things that fit our own preferred picture. We believe the Bible is true and that the picture it gives us will lead to a better scientific understanding of our earth. We have confidence that it will not lead a careful observer in the wrong direction. However, the Bible does not give many geological details, and thus we don't fully understand its puzzle picture—just as others don't fully understand their puzzle picture either. But each of these worldviews provides a compass, telling us where to look. The two compasses point in very different directions. The secret is to follow our compass and pray for God to open our eyes to see clearly what is there in the rocks, not allowing any assumptions to prevent us from discovering what is there.

While seeking to understand the difference between the two pictures, the biblical puzzle picture helps us recognize features it can lead us to—features that might not seem important in a naturalistic worldview. As you have heard about in this book, this process works. If the Bible is as reliable as we believe it is, we don't need to shun honest, open-minded research. It doesn't tell us ahead of time what our conclusions will be, but it can tell us: "Look over here, and you will find something interesting." It often leads us to discoveries that others could have made but did not because they were looking at the wrong puzzle picture. In each case, then, we must use careful scientific work to be sure our interpretations will stand up to objective evaluation. Our science must be at least as carefully done as anyone else's science.

We have never seen a global geological catastrophe in person, so how could we even know what evidence to look for? This is a genuine problem—one that for most scientists helps reinforce the bias toward interpreting geological evidence to fit the generally slow, more local processes we observe today. If we keep clearly in mind the two pictures, the two geological worldviews, it can help us overcome the biases and prevent careless thinking. I believe that even if we were wrong in some of our interpretations, science is benefited by persons with different perspectives engaged in serious research. Each person is apt to notice things that another might miss.

The approach to research we have described in these stories will only seem worthwhile to someone who is confident the Bible contains true communication from the great Creator of the universe. Solomon tells us, "The fear of the LORD is the beginning of wisdom, and knowledge of the Holy One is understanding" (Proverbs 9:10, NIV). Much evidence waits to be found and considered, but above all is the need for wisdom. When God responded to Job, what did He say? He didn't give answers to the difficult questions. He challenged humanity to remember how little we know in comparison to the God who created all and is Master and Redeemer of all. Where were we when the earth was created? Where were we when the rocks and fossils were formed? In the end, our choice of the worldview by which we evaluate ideas depends on wisdom. "The beginning of wisdom is this: Get wisdom. Though it cost you all you have, get understanding. Cherish her, and she will exalt you; embrace her, and she will honor you" (Proverbs

4:7, 8, NIV). This wisdom from God, if we accept it, will assist us in knowing which worldview should guide our lives and even our research.

Our research will not prove or disprove Creation or the Flood. Science doesn't provide proof in areas of such complexity, especially in the study of ancient events. However, research using a Bible-based worldview results in improved understanding of the rocks and fossils. Other scientists use their worldview, their theories, to suggest productive approaches to research—and we can do the same, with positive results. This will seem audacious and wild to many scientists, but I predict that a biblical worldview will ultimately result in better interpretations of geological history. I still don't have answers to many lines of evidence, but continued research opens up new insights not noticed before.

A whole world of this type of research is waiting for those who confidently pursue it. We don't need to be afraid of data, of diligent research. That we will suddenly see the whole picture clearly is unlikely. Our great God will open our eyes to see what we should learn at each step of the way. If Jesus Christ is our best friend and we trust Him fully, the search for new insights to which He will lead us is irresistible.

26

WHAT TO DO NEXT?

Conodonts, Milankovitch cycles, worm burrows, and stromatolites—I had studied these over the years. But what next? What step should I take to move toward answering our questions about how long it took to form the rocks?

The next several years were a continuing adventure of off-road trails and hard work on the barren, rocky Utah and Arizona hillsides. Diligence gradually brings insights, and the insights often come in unexpected ways.

We had begun the work in Utah as an exploratory project, seeking to understand what questions to ask and which mountains and rock outcrops held profitable research projects—projects that could answer our questions about the earth's history. As we explored, collected samples, and pondered the rocks, several research paths became clear. Working in Utah, we predicted that when we get our hands dirty and keep our eyes open and our minds receptive, God would lead us to productive ventures, and that prediction was being fulfilled.

Earlier in our research, I thought that God had led us to the first three research projects in which our biblical worldview offered valuable insights:

Coconino fossil trackways, Bridger turtles, and Peruvian whales. We were
not smart enough or knowledgeable enough to choose those specific projects ahead of time as examples of how our worldview can lead us. I still
think that is true, but during the later years of adventure in Utah, it seemed
that just about everywhere we looked, we saw puzzles that become more
clear when we begin with a biblical puzzle picture to guide us.

Our first Utah project had been taphonomy of conodonts, to help show
whether or not the meter-thick limestone beds were separate, individual
lime mudflows. Lots of work and sweat and adventure went into collecting
limestone samples for analysis. I had wondered if that was the project we
were looking for or if it was just a stepping-stone to better hypotheses. It
turned out to be the latter—a way to become familiar with the local geology and to find better research ideas to pursue. After having those precious
samples analyzed, it became evident to us that there are complications in
the study of conodont taphonomy that we could not solve. We still had
our questions about those distinct limestone layers, but we had to give
higher priority to other research ideas. The group that funded our work
understood this and continued to support our search for understanding.

Four projects got underway, and we had a list of others that we hope
students can work on. There is no end to fascinating opportunities for
wilderness pursuit of discovery, and life is too short for the task!

Those many layers of sedimentary rock with few fossil burrows were
beckoning, and Art Chadwick and I went back. We continued measuring
sections along hillsides and documenting the abundance of, or lack of,
burrows (bioturbation) in the bedded rock. After measuring thirty-four
sections all over Utah, our initial conclusions still stood—most of the rock
has few burrows, and there are not enough to obscure the distinct divisions
between layers of sediment. Only a few places are heavily burrowed. It is
hard to see how long time periods could have been involved in forming
these rock formations and still have so few burrows. We still needed to
measure more sections before publishing our findings. This work challenged some deeply held geological interpretations, and extraordinary
claims require extraordinary evidence to support them. We would continue

climbing hills with our noses close to the rock.

Along the way, a second geological question drew our attention. The question dealt with two rock formations I mentioned when we were doing helicopter aerial photography—the Moenkopi Formation and the Shinarump Conglomerate. After the Moenkopi mudstone was deposited, how long was it before the coarse Shinarump Conglomerate was deposited on top of it? Other geologists think it was ten to thirty million years. What does the evidence say?

The rocks forming the walls of the Grand Canyon are all in that part of the geological column known as the Paleozoic. The next formation above the top of the Grand Canyon is the Moenkopi Formation. The Moenkopi is found over at least 100,000 square miles in southern Utah and northern Arizona and nearby states. The sediment in the Moenkopi erodes away fairly easily, but it is often preserved because of the hard rock formation on top of it, the Shinarump Conglomerate. Since the Shinarump does not erode much, and the underlying Moenkopi is soft, they typically form a cliff with the Shinarump at the top of the cliff, preventing the Moenkopi from melting away.

How do you study rocks that form an inaccessible cliff hundreds of feet high? Art and I brought along Wayne, a friend who is skilled at flying drones. We searched for a part of the cliff that was close to the road and not too high for the use of our drone. The drone flew along the cliff, recording a video of the contact between the two rock formations. Part of the time, the drone was out of our sight, but our binoculars and the drone's camera view kept Wayne from crashing it into the cliff. That was helpful, but the drone was not strong enough to carry live geologists up along the cliff! Much of this research required the use of a helicopter that could fly us along the 100 miles of cliffs while we took several thousand photographs.

The photographs yielded much evidence and helped us find places where we could climb up the cliff to the top of the Moenkopi. This required an adventuresome spirit as we clambered over the steep places. At times, we also carefully avoided the rattlesnakes that kept track of our movements. We did some of this work in February, in temperatures that hovered around freezing. The previous week the weather forecast had predicted temperatures in the fifties, but when we got to Utah, the weather suddenly turned against us. We were joined by Doug, and the three of us somehow managed to keep from freezing up there on the hillsides.

In one place, the cliff was accessible only from the top. We drove our SUV for miles along an off-road trail and through the woods, getting as close as we could to the cliff. A few miles of walking brought us to a place where it was possible to scramble down a boulder pile through the Shinarump cliff. The partial snow cover kept us cautious, but we accomplished most of our plan. We began to ask ourselves, why hadn't we become molecular biologists, working in a warm laboratory? That would be more comfortable, but think of the awesome memories we would have missed.

The research papers we prepared would document evidence that is hard to explain unless the Moenkopi Formation formed rapidly and then was quickly covered by the Shinarump Conglomerate. It is unlikely we would have noticed this evidence if the conventional, millions-of-years geological theory had been controlling our mental framework.

A third project took us back to the stromatolites in the limestones of the House Range. Were they really stromatolites, formed by cyanobacteria that grew slowly as the limey sediment accumulated? They have features that do not look like stromatolites, but previous researchers have accepted them as stromatolites without question and without detailed study.

The limestone hills provide an abundant area for research on these structures, but you have to be careful of the jagged limestone surfaces. On one occasion, the limestone got the upper hand when I slipped and put a hand down to stop my fall. The limestone put a couple of nasty cuts on my hand. I was tempted to put some adhesive bandages on them and keep working, but the other two convinced me we should go to the little town of Delta, fifty miles away, for stitches. We called ahead, and the emergency room staff assured us they would be ready to care for the problem. We were amused at how eager they were, and so happy to have a real emergency to care for. It seems that they don't get many opportunities to practice their skills in this small town.

Over Sabbath, the weather turned ugly. We were just leaving camp in the

SUV when it began to hail, followed by heavy rain. We drove only about a quarter mile before the intense hail caused us to turn back to camp. We waited in the car, wondering when the one-inch-diameter hailstones would break our car windows. Finally it stopped, and we surveyed the damage. The hail had destroyed a couple of tents and driven dents into our vehicle and the sides of the chuck wagon.

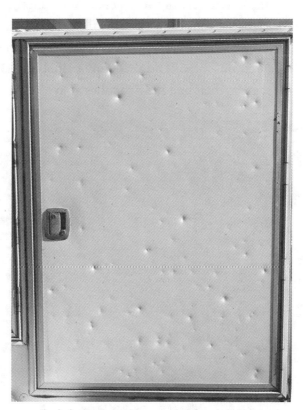

The chuckwagon door with numerous dents from the hailstorm.

The next day we drove to another mountain range about forty miles from camp. The heavy rain had eroded ditches across the dirt "roads," and piles of hailstones revealed the areas subject to the hailstorm. It was obvious the rain had affected the whole forty-mile region, but the hail was only in an area about a mile wide, centered on our camp. Perhaps someone didn't like us being there!

Out in the House Range, we used our high-precision GPS equipment to map the presumed stromatolites over several hundred square miles. They are present at more than one elevational level, or stratigraphic level. At one level, we stumbled across a large patch of structures that were exactly like the other stromatolites, except for some unique features. It was a field of very elongated stromatolite-like structures, packed tightly together, and all oriented in the same direction. Later that day I was two miles away, on another hilltop, and found another patch of the same elongated structures. I took out my compass and checked the direction of their orientation. It was exactly the same as the other patch. What did this mean? Did these tiny cyanobacteria decide they would orient the same as their buddies two miles away?

Art Chadwick and a student set up the
high-precision GPS that was a valuable research tool.

A few weeks of research revealed many of these fields of elongated structures all over the House Range, and they were are all oriented the same way, which happens to be the same direction as the many earthquake faults in this range of hills. *There is something intriguing going on here*, I thought, *and it is unlikely that it was determined by any cyanobacteria*. Were these really stromatolites, or had we discovered some other phenomenon? As I write this, the Utah project is on the back burner for a couple of years while we finish up other research, but we plan to return to the House Range.

The fourth project takes us to Arizona, to the Coconino Sandstone, to finish that work (if research ever really gets finished!). With a couple of graduate students working on the Coconino, it seems like a good time to pursue this project to some kind of end point.

Back at the Coconino Sandstone, taking notes
after drilling a core out of the sandstone.

For decades geologists have cited the Coconino as a classic example of an eolian, desert sand accumulation (*eolian* means formed by wind, in a desert). But almost nobody comes here and does research on the Coconino SS. That is probably why our extensive searching began to reveal features in the sandstone that had never been described in the geological literature. There are small ridges and folds and other deformed structures in the otherwise smooth sandstone surfaces. These are called soft-sediment deformation, formed before the sand became cemented into sandstone. There are other features that, like the soft-sediment deformation, look suspiciously like the results of seismic (earthquake) events disturbing the sand deposit. Again, as I write this, we are preparing several manuscripts to be submitted for publication in geology journals.

Besides these new features, there is accumulating evidence that does not look like what is expected if the Coconino sand was deposited in a desert.

Our next task would be to prepare to submit these ideas to a research journal and see if we can convince our geological colleagues to reconsider their cherished eolian interpretation of the Coconino SS. Unlike many other geologists, we pray for wisdom to understand the rocks and for success in publishing our conclusions.

Graduate student taking notes on one of the sloping cross-beds
of the Coconino Sandstone at Ash Fork, Arizona.

This is not the end of a book but the beginning of more adventure and the next steps in the search for understanding. Neither Harold Coffin nor I ever dreamed of the winding, fascinating path that would result from his simple request in 1971 for me to read a few papers on fossil trackways. Art Chadwick and I and our collaborators hope others will join us and accomplish more than we can do in our short lifetimes. God blesses our efforts when we make Him our leader!

Afterword

FOUNDATION FOR A LIFE

W hat was it that led me in the direction I took and led to the adventures recounted in the preceding chapters? What prepared me for this work?

For anything worthwhile I've accomplished in my life, much of the credit goes to my wise father. He was a farmer, and later a maintenance man, and thus would not be considered by modern society as a great man, but I know better. He shared with me the following values:

- Work hard and always do your very best.
- Be on time.
- Do your work carefully.
- Don't be satisfied to do things the way everyone else does if you can find a better way.

My father did and said things to give me confidence. On the farms in Kansas, where I grew up, kids learned to drive trucks and tractors as soon as they could reach the pedals, and I was tall for my age. One day, at the age of 11, I sat under the Osage orange trees and watched Dad driving the tractor with a rake to bring mowed alfalfa into rows for baling in a forty-acre field. He drove over to where I was and said he needed to do some other work and would like for me to finish the raking. I reminded him that I knew how to drive the tractor but had never used the tractor-drawn rake. He showed me how the controls worked and walked away. I knew him well enough to know that he wouldn't walk away because he didn't care but to show me that he had confidence I could do the job. After finishing the raking and looking back over the field, I realized that my rows were as straight as his. The scene, with its feelings of satisfaction, comes back to me now as if it occurred yesterday.

My father lived a life that said, "Have confidence, but keep it subject to God and His Word." He was glad to invest in experiences that prepared his kids for life and teach us useful skills. When it was time for me to visit colleges and choose one, I found out that my college of choice taught house construction by building small model houses to scale, with little scaled-down rafters, studs, and other lumber. After seeing this on a visit to the college with Dad, I wanted to build such a house. Dad bought a book on building houses, we borrowed a table saw, and I built my scaled-down house, three feet long, with everything put together like a real house. This, and a summer working with two cousins who were contractors, gave me the courage to later design and build my own house.

Growing up on the farm, though there was time for play, everyone did their share of the work. Sometimes I would have preferred to play more, but I was also conscious that I was driving tractors in the field when my city friends were not long past graduating from their tricycles. We were not rich, and it was necessary for me to work all during secondary school and college to help pay the bills. There were various repetitive and occasionally boring jobs, but it made them more interesting to compete against myself to see how fast the job could be done without any sacrifices in the quality of the work. All that experience painting broom handles, milking cows, labeling cans of food in a factory, and janitorial work also built confidence that I could make my way in life and taught me many practical skills that were valuable even in scientific research.

Dad gave me the freedom to choose a career that fit my interests and abilities. As a student in college and graduate school, I didn't start out in geology but studied biology. A summer of travel around the US and Canada, along with taking an ornithology class and collecting small mammals, yielded firsthand experience in all the major life zones—a valuable asset in future research. A few years later, I began to train in geology and paleontology. This meant a lot of extra time and classes, but that was actually an ideal sequence of education. The biology background was valuable for understanding fossils and ancient environments.

There is a particular advantage to beginning in one field of study and then changing to another. A scientist learns, in graduate school, two basic things: (1) how to think like a scientist and critically evaluate ideas, while (2) also learning many concepts in his/her field of education. Those concepts are learned, and probably accepted, before one can fully understand how to think critically. But then changing fields requires the person to encounter the concepts in their new field after having gained experience in careful and critical thought. This facilitates more original and creative thinking in the person's new field.

There were other broadening experiences for me. For thirty years, I attended a yearly meeting of scientists, theologians, and others to discuss science and faith issues. The meetings were always at some geologically instructive area, with field trips. This meant hearing and participating in discussions every year among the most skilled professionals, learning how they handled the relationship between the Bible, geology, and aspects of evolutionary science. Similar gatherings continued after the thirty years, always fostering an active stream of feedback on this topic.

Perhaps best of all, my father modeled ways to do things in the best way possible. For some years we raised five thousand turkeys on the farm each year. For most farmers, this meant keeping the birds in a small enclosure and fattening them on commercial turkey feed. Dad didn't see how that would result in healthy birds, so each year he prepared a forty-acre field with alfalfa or a similar crop the turkeys could eat. After the turkey chicks were big enough, we took them, their shelters, and food dispensers to the field, and they lived the way turkeys should live. It was a lot of work, and someone had to sleep with the turkeys every single night to keep the coyotes at bay, but for Dad it was worth it all when the meat company said these were the healthiest turkeys raised in Kansas. That's how I learned to do the science that I do.

REFERENCES

Below are selected references to published papers resulting from the research described or mentioned in this book. All except the paper on dinosaur and human footprints are in pccr-rcvicwcd scientific research journals. Also listed are some of my books on the topic of origins.

Journals

Brand, Leonard R. "Field and Laboratory Studies on the Coconino Sandstone (Permian) Vertebrate Footprints and Their Paleoecological Implications." *Palaeogeography, Palaeoclimatology, Palaeoecology* 28 (1979): 25–38. https://doi.org/10.1016/0031-0182(79)90111-1.

———. "An Improved High-Precision Jacob's Staff Design." *Journal of Sedimentary Research, Section A: Sedimentary Petrology and Processes* 65, no. 3a (July 1995): 561. https://doi.org/10.2110/jsr.65.561.

———. "Lacustrine Deposition in the Bridger Formation: Lake Gosiute Extended." *The Mountain Geologist* 44, no. 2 (April 2007): 69–78.

———. "Variations in Salamander Trackways Resulting From Substrate

Differences." *Journal of Paleontology* 70, no. 6 (1996): 1004–1010.
https://doi.org/10.1017/S0022336000038701.

Brand, Leonard R., and Gilbert Dupper. "Dental Impression Materials
Useful for Making Molds of Fossils." *Journal of Paleontology* 56, no. 5
(September 1982): 1305–1307.

Brand, Leonard R., Raúl Esperante, Arthur V. Chadwick, Orlando Poma
Porras, and Merling Alomía. "Fossil Whale Preservation Implies High
Diatom Accumulation Rate in the Miocene-Pliocene Pisco Formation
of Peru." *Geology* 32, no. 2 (2004): 165–168. https://doi.org/10.1130/
G20079.1.

Brand, Leonard R., H. Thomas Goodwin, Peter D. Ambrose, and H.
Paul Buchheim. "Taphonomy of Turtles in the Middle Eocene Bridger
Formation, SW Wyoming." *Palaeogeography, Palaeoclimatology, Palaeoecology* 162, no. 1–2 (September 15, 2000): 171–189. https://doi.org/10
.1016/S0031-0182(00)00111-5.

Brand, Leonard R., Michael Hussey, and John Taylor. "Decay and Disarticulation of Small Vertebrates in Controlled Experiments." *Journal of
Taphonomy* 1, no. 2 (2003): 69–95.

———. "Taphonomy of Freshwater Turtles: Decay and Disarticulation
in Controlled Experiments." *Journal of Taphonomy* 1, no. 4 (2003):
233–245.

Brand, Leonard R., and Thu Tang. "Fossil Vertebrate Footprints in the
Coconino Sandstone (Permian) of Northern Arizona: Evidence for
Underwater Origin." *Geology* 19, no. 12 (1991): 1201–1204. https://
doi.org/10.1130/0091-7613(1991)019<1201:FVFITC>2.3.CO;2.

Brand, Leonard R., Mario Urbina, Arthur V. Chadwick, Thomas J.
DeVries, and Raúl Esperante. "A High Resolution Stratigraphic Framework for the Remarkable Fossil Cetacean Assemblage of the Miocene/
Pliocene Pisco Formation, Peru." *Journal of South American Earth Sciences*
31, no. 4 (April 2011): 414–425. https://doi.org/10.1016/j.jsames.2011
.02.015.

Brand, Leonard R., Mingmin Wang, and Arthur V. Chadwick. "Global
Database of Paleocurrent Trends Through the Phanerozoic and

Precambrian." *Scientific Data* 2, 150025 (2015). https://doi.org/10 .1038/sdata.2015.25. Metadata is available at http://www.nature.com /sdata/.

Buchheim, H. Paul, Leonard R. Brand, and H. Thomas Goodwin. "Lacustrine to Fluvial Floodplain Deposition in the Eocene Bridger Formation." *Palaeogeography, Palaeoclimatology, Palaeoecology* 162, no. 1–2 (September 15, 2000): 191–209. https://doi.org/10.1016/S0031-0182(00)00112-7.

Coulson, Ken P., and Leonard R. Brand. "Lithistid Sponge-Microbial Reef-Building Communities Construct Laminated, Upper Cambrian (Furongian) 'Stromatolites.' " *Palaios* 31, no. 7 (2016): 358–370. http:// dx.doi.org/10.2110/palo.2016.029.

Coulson, Ken P., Leonard R. Brand, and Arthur V. Chadwick. "Microbialite Elongation by Means of Coalescence: An Example From the Middle Furongian (Upper Cambrian) Notch Peak Formation of Western Utah." *Facies* 62, no. 3 (2016): 1–17. https://doi.org/10.1007 /s10347-016-0469-5.

Esperante, Raúl, Leonard R. Brand, Arthur V. Chadwick, and Orlando Poma Porras. "Taphonomy and Paleoenvironmental Conditions of Deposition of Fossil Whales in the Diatomaceous Sediments of the Miocene/Pliocene Pisco Formation, Southern Peru—A New Fossil-Lagerstätte." *Palaeogeography, Palaeoclimatology, Palaeoecology* 417 (January 1, 2015): 337–370. https://doi.org/10.1016/j.palaeo.2014 .09.029.

———. "Taphonomy of Fossil Whales in the Diatomaceous Sediments of the Miocene/Pliocene Pisco Formation, Peru." In *Current Topics on Taphonomy and Fossilization*, edited by Miquel de Renzi, Miguel Vicente Pardo Alonso, Margarita Belinchón, E. Peñalver, P. Montoya, and Ana Márquez-Aliaga, 337–343. Valencia, Spain: Ayuntamiento de Valencia, 2002.

Esperante, Raúl, Leonard R. Brand, Kevin E. Nick, Orlando Poma Porras, and Mario Urbina. "Exceptional Occurrence of Fossil Baleen in Shallow Marine Sediments of the Neogene Pisco Formation, Southern Peru." *Palaeogeography, Palaeoclimatology, Palaeoecology* 257, no. 3 (January 23,

2008): 344–360. https://doi.org/10.1016/j.palaeo.2007.11.001.

Kennedy, E. G., R. Kablanow, and Arthur V. Chadwick. "Evidence for Deep Water Deposition of the Tapeats Sandstone, Grand Canyon, Arizona." Proceedings of Third Biennual Conference of Research on the Colorado Plateau, edited by C. Van Riper III and E. T. Deshler, US Dept. of Interior. *Transactions and Proceedings Series NPS/NRNAN/NRTP* 97, no. 12 (1997): 215–228.

Lockley, Martin G., David B. Loope, and Leonard R. Brand. "Comment and Reply on 'Fossil Vertebrate Footprints in the Coconino Sandstone (Permian) of Northern Arizona: Evidence for Underwater Origin.' " *Geology* 20, no. 7 (1992): 666–670. https://doi .org/10.1130/0091-7613(1992)020<0666:CAROFV>2.3.CO;2.

McLain, Matthew A., David Nelsen, Keith Snyder, Christopher T. Griffin, Bethania Siviero, Leonard R. Brand, and Arthur V. Chadwick. "Tyrannosaur Cannibalism: A Case of a Tooth-Traced Tyrannosaurid Bone in the Lance Formation (Maastrichtian), Wyoming." *Palaios* 33, no. 4 (2018): 164–173, http://dx.doi.org/10.2110/palo.2017.076.

Neufeld, Berney R. "Dinosaur Tracks and Giant Men." *Origins* 2, no. 2 (1975): 64–76.

Completed and available privately:

Brand, Leonard. "Current Research: Taphonomy of Fossil Turtles, Sedimentology, and Geological Mapping of the Eocene Bridger Formation, SW Wyoming: Mapping of Bridger Unit B." http://ftp.llu.edu/lbrand /research-bridger.html.

Books

Brand, Leonard. *Creation? Really? A Conversation on Origins.* Nampa, ID: Pacific Press®, 2019.

———. *Genesis and Science: Where Is the Evidence Going?* Nampa, ID: Pacific Press®, forthcoming.

Brand, Leonard, and Arthur Chadwick. *Faith, Reason, and Earth History: A Paradigm of Earth and Biological Origins by Intelligent Design.* 3rd ed.

Berrien Springs, MI: Andrews University Press, 2016.

Brand, Leonard, and Richard M. Davidson. *Choose You This Day: Why It Matters What You Believe About Creation*. Nampa, ID: Pacific Press®, 2013.

Brand, Leonard, with Anita Oliver. *God, Science, Friends and God's Love for You*. Nampa, ID: Pacific Press®, 2019.